Getting the Buggers into Science

Also available from Continuum:

Sue Cowley: *Letting the Buggers be Creative*

Christine Farmery: *Teaching Science 3–11*

Also available in the series:

Mike Ollerton: *Getting the Buggers to Add Up*

Sue Cowley: *Getting the Buggers to Behave 2*

Barbara Ward: *Getting the Buggers to Draw*

Amanda Barton: *Getting the Buggers into Languages*

Sue Cowley: *Getting the Buggers to Think*

Ian McCormack: *Getting the Buggers to Turn Up*

Sue Cowley: *Getting the Buggers to Write 2*

Getting the Buggers into Science

Christine Farmery

continuum
LONDON • NEW YORK

Continuum International Publishing Group

The Tower Building   15 East 26th Street

11 York Road   New York

London SE1 7NX   NY 10010

www.continuumbooks.com

British Library Cataloguing-in-Publication Data

A catalogue record for this book is available from the British Library.

ISBN 0–8264–7397–0 (paperback)

Typeset by BookEns Ltd, Royston, Herts.
Printed and bound in Great Britain by Cromwell Press,
Trowbridge, Wiltshire

This book is dedicated
to the grown-up children in my life:
my son Ian Farmery and my daughter Ruth Farmery.

Contents

List of figures

Acknowledgements

Thank you to everyone who has inspired me in science over the years. Special thanks to Christina and Alexandra at Continuum for their faith and encouragement in my writing.

Introduction

Science is an important area for our children to study; not only is it a core subject in the National Curriculum for England and Wales, and so is to be studied in depth by children from the age of 5, but also it can be an extremely motivating subject for even the most reluctant learner. On the other hand, it could be argued that, unlike English and maths, science may not be of use to our children in adulthood, hence it is open to question why it should be studied at all! Thus, unless a convincing justification for the importance of science study is made, the motivation and inspiration I believe it can provide for reluctant learners are that much harder to supply. The aim of this book is therefore to provide such a justification and to offer ideas to encourage children not only to engage in scientific activity but also to instigate their own investigations and research.

The material in this book will be of use to teachers across the primary and secondary age range and will both establish a rationale for science teaching and provide ideas for getting scientific activities and scientific enquiry going within the classroom. The aim of the book is to provide a useful and practical resource that is based on my own ideas on science teaching and my experiences in the classroom. I have set out to explain how and why I think science can be interesting and relevant to all learners, using some of my favourite activities that I have used with different sets of pupils to illustrate my ideas. The scope of the book means that I have only been able to include some of my very favourite activities; there are obviously many, many more ideas to be found and used in the ways that I am suggesting. The best ideas are going to be those that you devise or adapt for yourself.

I cannot claim many of the ideas I have included as being original; writers, deliverers of courses and colleagues have all inspired me and helped shape the ideas of science I now hold and the activities I regularly use in my teaching. To all those people who have inspired the activities that I am presenting within the book (and me) – thank you. Where I can remember the source of the activity, I have acknowledged this within the book, but for many of the activities I have not been able to do this as I cannot remember how I came to use the idea or what inspired me to try it out with my pupils.

The book offers some ideas of the nature and practice of science teaching but is intended to be neither a book on the theory of science nor a collection of age-appropriate lesson plans. I have included what I believe to be the justification for teaching science to our children, together with hints, tips, examples and teaching strategies that I have used in my teaching and that may motivate your students. I do not always present science to the children I teach in a recognized *scientific approach*, and so have also included some of the more unusual ideas, contexts and strategies that I have used with a range of pupils, including the more reluctant learners.

The book touches on a range of considerations within science teaching, from getting science going to looking at science beyond the curriculum. I therefore do not concentrate solely on ideas for weekly science lessons but show how science can involve everyone, can be adapted to cater for all – from the low-ability pupil to the gifted pupil – and can be studied throughout the school day and beyond. I also include ideas for where scientific activity can support the whole curriculum by providing the context for learning in a number of other subjects. Again, although the ideas suggested may be used as presented here, I hope they will inspire you to look for many other opportunities to use science across the curriculum in your school or setting. I have also included a section on assessing the performance of your pupils, as assessment can be used to motivate and inspire even the most reluctant of learners.

Throughout the book I use an informal and straightforward way of writing about science and science teaching, as I believe it is important to accept science as an everyday subject rather than one that is overcomplicated with specific vocabulary that needs to be interpreted, and yet occasionally the use of technical vocabulary is unavoidable. Therefore, where I have used scientific terminology there is an explanation of this alongside the ideas presented. This style of writing is used to enable everyone, whether specialists in science or not, to access the material in the book and to present it to their pupils without first having to work out what it all means! My hope is that you are able to use the book to develop both your own understanding, and that of the pupils you teach, of what science and science teaching are all about, and to establish meaningful science and scientific enquiry in your classroom.

Part One

Setting the Scene

1 What is science?

It is interesting that a book about motivating pupils into science and science study must first begin with a definition of what science is. The study of science is a requirement of the National Curriculum of England and Wales, and yet the subject still conjures up an air of mystery – for children and adults alike. I have developed a passion for science and science teaching in the primary school by teaching it as a stand-alone subject, through other subjects and using non-scientific contexts, and believe firmly that the scientific thinking the pupils have engaged in is just as valid as that of the greatest of scientists. I justify this by relating the science thinking of pupils to that of two particular scientists, Archimedes and Newton, to show that the scientific thinking my pupils are engaged in is not so far removed from theirs, which arose supposedly through the non-scientific pastimes of taking a bath and sitting under a tree! This relation is central to the rest of the book: my approach is to explore what constitutes *science* and not merely to consider the study in terms of a set of skills and knowledge to be acquired. Science is so much more than this: it is also a way of working and thinking, and so this chapter looks first at recognizing and identifying scientific activity, and then at the importance of its study.

Towards a definition for science

My own book *Teaching Science 3–11: The Essential Guide* (Farmery 2002) began with this same question: What is science? Although primary science is a subject I have studied at University (the main subject of my BEd degree) and a passion of mine, I found dealing with this question to be the hardest part of that book to write! I found it so difficult to put into words what made up this subject I was so fanatical about, and yet if I couldn't begin to define science, then how could I write an essential book about the subject? I began to look at the definitions for science from different sources and used them to work towards a definition that I was comfortable with. The process began with the dictionary definition of science as 'systematic and formulated knowledge' that is 'based mainly on observation, experiment and induction' (*The Concise Oxford Dictionary* 1982, p. 939). The *Concise Oxford*'s definition reflects the traditional identification of science as a subject consisting of the interrelated disciplines of *knowledge* and *skills*, but I believed that science involves so much more than this. I wanted the definition to include the way of working and thinking that I believe science indicates – the organized and logical steps that are needed and the thinking behind the practical activity. Through further reading to justify my beliefs, the term *attitudes* – both scientific attitudes and attitudes towards science – became important, and I realized that it is these attitudes that bring science as a subject alive for me.

It was the identification of *attitudes* that confirmed the inclusion, within the definition of science, of a way of thinking and working. Scientific attitudes were acknowledged as including curiosity, asking questions, seeking answers, working through problems and arriving at conclusions – all of which indicate the need for logical thought and a systematic way of working. The notion of attitudes towards science, particularly positive ones, was noted as essential for adults living in a technological and scientific world.

The definition of science I believe in then began to take shape. It included the need for the learner to develop his or her own ideas, attitudes and interpretations, and science for me is consequently a much wider subject than one that simply involves acquiring a set of skills and knowledge. I do not deny that science skills and knowledge are important, but what I believe in is a definition of science and science study that is based on the interplay of:

- a body of knowledge;
- the skills used in the development of knowledge;
- the thinking that provides the interpretation of the evidence;

- the understanding the discovery of the knowledge leads to;
- the attitudes that the learning develops.

What makes an activity scientific?

My understanding of what science is demonstrates how wide the subject of science and its study can be, and so it can be appreciated that not all the aspects of science listed will be studied at the same time. The aspects may have to be covered in isolation and then linked together at a later stage; it is therefore not surprising that scientific activity is often portrayed as learning, and remembering, a set of science facts and the acquisition of a series of science skills. It is this view of science that may discourage some learners from engaging in science study, and so it is important that science in school is portrayed as exciting, interesting and relevant. I have already stated that I have taught science using non-scientific contexts, and yet the science the pupils were involved in was important for their understanding and for coverage of the science curriculum. I originally chose to teach some science through these contexts to engage and enthuse the learners, and to demonstrate the relevance of science study to the interests of the pupils. In order to do this, I needed to be able to identify the science learning the different activities could provide.

If we use the definition for science given above, then we see that an activity may be classed as scientific if it involves the development of scientific knowledge, the development or use of scientific skills, the development of the learner's own ideas in science or the development of attitudes, or if it provokes scientific thought and interpretations. Quite a list! It can now be appreciated how wide-ranging the activities that fit this definition may be, and why so many activities can be identified. The key for teachers is to be able to justify their choice of activity in terms of the science learning it promotes. This approach to scientific study acknowledges that knowledge and skills are important to science as a whole, and recognizes that science teaching is not simply the teacher instructing the learner, while ensuring the significance of discovery, thought, interpretation and discussion. Science, and its study, is therefore an active process in all respects. It is by using this explanation of science that the teacher will be able to identify a range of relevant and exciting scientific activities that involve the full range of the aspects of science.

The teacher's role in effective teaching and learning in science therefore begins with the collation of a range of activities that are exciting and relevant, that individually promote at least one aspect of what constitutes science and that steer the learner through the science curriculum being offered. Quite a tall order! What is contained within the rest of the book is written to assist teachers in their quest to deliver exciting and relevant activities that motivate all learners.

Thinking and working like a scientist

To be able to use the skills of science – to work systematically, to investigate and develop ideas – indicates the need for pupils to be able to work and think like scientists themselves, and yet they may know little of the lives of scientists. The simplest way to inform pupils about the life and work of a scientist is to read stories concerning a range of scientists, both well-known scientists from the past and present, and more unfamiliar ones. By introducing your pupils to these true stories you will provide them with the real-life backgrounds to how different scientists live and work, or lived and worked. The subsequent relating of the work your pupils carry out to that of real scientists can be particularly motivating for reluctant learners, as it provides a meaning for their work. This identification of a purpose for learning is a recurring theme throughout the book, as I believe many of today's learners learn best when they feel they have a reason to do so – reluctant learners particularly.

The stories of scientists can be used in many ways in the classroom, not only as a context for their own work but also:

- to enable the pupils to appreciate how scientists' discoveries are made;
- to show them how scientists collect evidence and use it to provide the basis for the establishment of new theories in science;

- to consolidate in them an understanding of how scientists work;
- to recreate the simple investigations scientists have carried out;
- to encourage pupils to try out science ideas presented as known facts;
- to encourage pupils to investigate their own ideas in science;
- to set scientific knowledge and understanding in context.

The development of scientific skills is therefore important because it enables pupils to carry out this range of activities. It can be appreciated through this list that we wish our pupils to think and work like scientists: to recreate the investigations of scientists, where we know what the outcome should be; to try out their own ideas, where the outcomes are unknown; and to *prove* the validity of a scientific fact or idea. The emphasis on thinking and interpreting, rather than merely memorizing scientific facts, makes science accessible for all pupils, including both reluctant learners and less able pupils. As it includes recognition of the learner's own ideas, and does not rely solely on the recall of *correct* knowledge, science is a much less threatening subject than it was once assumed to be! It is not enough to simply recall a set of facts; it is important to understand how that knowledge came to be discovered and accepted.

A British scientist: Winnie-the-Pooh

There are many stories of scientists easily accessible in books and on the Internet. I will include the stories of three particular scientists later in the book – Christian Doppler in Chapter 5, Ben Franklin in Chapter 8 and Maria Mitchell in Chapter 12 – together with ideas for using the stories with pupils, but there are other stories you can use, particularly with the younger pupils. I first heard the story of how Winnie-the-Pooh invented a new game used to demonstrate the skills and thoughts of a scientist at a briefing meeting about science clubs for children and was inspired by the message that anyone can be a scientist and that science is evident in even the most everyday of activities.

Pooh invents a new game

Here is a myst'ry
About a little fir tree.
Owl says it's his tree,
And Kanga says it's her tree.

'Which doesn't make sense,' said Pooh, 'because Kanga doesn't live in a tree.'   He had just come to the bridge; and not looking where he was going, he tripped over something, and the fir-cone jerked out of his paw into the river.

'Bother,' said Pooh, as it floated slowly under the bridge, and he went back to get another fir-cone which had a rhyme to it. But then he thought that he would just look at the river instead, because it was a peaceful sort of day, so he lay down and looked at it, and it slipped slowly away beneath him ... and suddenly, there was his fir-cone slipping away too.

'That's funny,' said Pooh. 'I dropped it on the other side,' said Pooh, 'and it came out this side! I wonder if it would do it again?' And he went back for some more fir-cones.

It did. It kept on doing it. Then he dropped two in at once, and leant over the bridge to see which of them would come out first: and one of them did; but as they were both the same size, he didn't know if it was the one which he wanted to win, or the other one. So the next time he dropped one big one and one little one, and the big one came out first, which was what he had said it would do, and the little one came out last, which was what he had said it would do, so he had won twice ... and when he went home for tea, he had won thirty-six and lost twenty-eight, which meant that he was – that he had – well, you take twenty-eight from thirty-six, and *that's* what he was. Instead of the other way round.

And that was the beginning of the game called Poohsticks, which Pooh invented, and which he and his friends used to play on the edge of the Forest. But they played with sticks instead of fir-cones, because they were easier to mark.

A. A. Milne

Within the story, Winnie-the-Pooh used many scientific skills and scientific thinking in the invention of his new game. Here are the ones I have identified below, but you may be able to identify more:

- *Observation* – when the fir-cone jerked out of his paw into the river and floated downstream.
- *Reflection* – on what had happened to the fir-cone, and how it wasn't what he would have expected.
- *Questioning* – using his reflection on what had happened, he asked a question that could be investigated: 'I dropped it on the other side ... and it came out this side! I wonder if it would do it again?'
- *Investigation* – testing his theory.
- *Repeating observations* – repeatedly dropping the fir-cones in the water.
- *Refining the investigation* – dropping two cones in at once.
- *Reflecting on his way of working* – realizing he couldn't tell which fir-cone had come out from under the bridge first.
- *Refining the investigation again* – using two different-sized cones.
- *Prediction* – predicting the larger cone would come out from under the bridge first.
- *Relating results to the prediction* – stating that '... the big one came out first, which was what he had said it would do'.
- *Refined the investigation again* – using sticks instead of fir-cones, because they were easier to mark.

I think this is a perfect example of how a scientist thinks and works! Winnie-the-Pooh sees what is really an everyday event, questions why the event is happening and then sets out to answer his own question. The investigation was used not solely to identify facts but also to develop knowledge through the testing of an idea, gathering of evidence and the all-important interpretation of the evidence to generate theory. This is surely the true essence of science.

The story can be used with pupils in many ways:

- to illustrate the skills of scientific enquiry;
- to demonstrate how a simple, everyday activity uses scientific skills;

- to illustrate the thought processes of scientific enquiry;
- to demonstrate how evidence needs to be interpreted;
- to suggest further investigations into objects in water.

The list goes on!

Cinderella

Another story I have used to illustrate the skills and thoughts of a scientist is that of *Cinderella*. Although there are many versions of the story, all agree that Cinderella's stepsisters ridiculed her and caused her misery. Some versions report that one day the stepsisters added to her workload, as she seemed to do all the work around the house, by scattering peas and lentils into the ashes in the fireplace, so that she had to spend the whole day sorting them out again. I have not seen it explained how she did this but she may have used a series of sieves to separate the three solids. The skills she used may be identified in the same way as above. She had a problem to solve: the problem of separating peas, lentils and ash. She may have used prior knowledge; as she did all the cooking she would have had knowledge of sieving and the use of different-sized sieves, and could have used the skills of investigation to plan and carry out the work in a logical order, resulting in the separation of the three solids. Cinderella is therefore also a great scientist!

The above are two of my favourite stories for identifying scientists at work, I'm sure you will be able to think of many more. The key is to consider the scientific skills, knowledge, thought and/or interpretation indicated in the stories. Another of my favourites is the Aesop fable 'The Crow and the Water Pot'. In this story the crow finds a water pot with some water in it but cannot reach down to the surface of the water with his beak. After thinking about the problem, and using previous knowledge, he dropped pebble after pebble into the pitcher until the water level rose sufficiently for him to drink the water. Try to list the skills and knowledge the crow used to solve his problem and you'll see how easy it is to identify appropriate stories.

Why is the study of science important?

When the National Curriculum was first introduced, science was one of three core subjects (alongside English and maths), and, despite numerous reviews since, it continues to retain this status. When one considers why English and maths are important to study, their application through both childhood and adulthood is easy to see. Children read, write and use mathematical skills in almost all subjects across the curriculum, and adults use some aspect of English and maths on a daily basis, from reading the morning paper to filling in a form, from paying for goods to working out a bus timetable. In contrast, the application of science is not so easy to discern. It cannot be justified solely in terms of the technological age we live in, as many of the appliances we use do not require knowledge of the science behind the invention. It can therefore be appreciated how engaging the reluctant learner is all the more difficult when the rationale for studying the subject is not immediately obvious. Yet there are numerous reasons why the study of science is important to both the child and the adult.

- Scientific skills are transferable across the curriculum and relate well to adult life. These include the skills of thinking, playing with ideas, trying out ideas, finding out, asking questions, reflecting, predicting, linking ideas and developing an understanding of cause and effect.
- Science study often requires the pupil to search for information, another skill that can be used across the curriculum and into adult life.
- Scientific enquiry encourages critical thinking about the world by using observation, evidence, logic and reasoning to develop understanding.
- Environmental awareness can be developed through the study of environmental issues.
- Science study develops the skills of communication – from discussing science and scientific discoveries to presenting information about one's own ideas to others.
- Knowledge of scientific language is needed in order to fully understand and question the effects of science in terms of discoveries, inventions and technologies.

- The stories of scientists, inventors and inventions enable pupils to consider the importance of science to their everyday life and to life worldwide.
- Science is an imaginative subject involving the need to provide explanations for the results of scientific enquiry, and so requires pupils to be able to think through their ideas and interpretations.
- Science study in school ensures that the ideas concerning the world that pupils develop are arrived at through a planned, relevant and organized science curriculum.

These reasons for studying science demonstrate clearly that it is the skills and attitudes that will be taken into adult life, rather than the recall of popular facts. It is a well-known scientific *fact* that 'plants take in carbon dioxide and give out oxygen'. To know this does not require a detailed understanding of the process of photosynthesis, and yet we accept it as true. Why do we accept this? Why do we accept what scientists claim to be true? By understanding how the knowledge is arrived at and how the scientific community came to accept the ideas as true is important to our acceptance of the *fact*. It is this aspect of science that makes its study important for pupils in their adult life, in order for them to understand how and why science impacts on their everyday lives, and to be able to accept or question new discoveries as they occur.

2 Attitudes to science

So far I have concentrated on the development of scientific attitudes – the attitudes of curiosity, asking questions, working through problems and arriving at conclusions – and their importance for the study of science. Of equal, if not more, importance is the development of attitudes *towards* science. These too are vitally important to the study of science and contribute to the reason for its study. It has been noted (Hodgson and Scanlon, 1985) that a child's attitudes towards science are shaped very early in his or her life, and that the most significant features in determining the type of attitudes formed towards science are the teaching styles used by the teacher *and* the teacher's own image of science. It can therefore be appreciated that when a teacher is working with reluctant learners, the attitudes towards science that he or she holds are of paramount importance. In order to engage the learners it is crucial that the teacher is confident and enthusiastic about teaching and learning in science in order to inspire the pupil, and yet many adults have negative attitudes towards science themselves. This book is therefore written for both the teacher and the pupil, to provide inspiration for the teacher if needed and to enthuse the pupil. The ideas regarding science and its importance to study are, for that reason, also important for teachers to fully consider their own attitudes towards science; this is essential if teachers are to be confident and enthusiastic about science and science teaching.

Teacher attitudes

It is a fact that many adults, including teachers, have negative views about teaching and learning in science; these views are often related to our own experiences of science education and a belief that we can't understand science ourselves! However, I fully agree with Harlen (1992) that the main requirement for successful teaching in science is to have a *feel* for what it is. The ideas presented in this book will, I hope, enable you to develop a feel for what science and scientific activity are, and to challenge any ideas you may have held previously about the subject being based on a body of knowledge to be learned and a set of skills to be used to arrive at the answer the teacher wanted. Developing positive attitudes towards science as an adult may be quite daunting, depending on your previous experiences and attitudes, and yet, although this may be a difficult journey for you to embark upon, it will be rewarding in terms of your science teaching and in terms of the experiences you provide for your learners. This book is merely a starting point; in addition to the ideas presented here there are many other sources of inspiration for you to use to develop your own attitudes towards science. These sources include the many science activity centres that are open to the public, science museums, children's television programmes and both children's and teachers' science websites on the Internet.

Pupils' attitudes

Science appears to be intrinsically fascinating to children; even the word itself appears to interest children! Science is all around us and seems to feature in the news almost daily. In addition, children's television programmes often include a segment of science, and so science itself does not have either the air of mystery or the image of being boring that it once had. Pupils' experiences of science beyond school are usually exciting and interesting, seemingly out of the ordinary yet relevant at the same time; and yet a pupil's expectation of school science study often does not reflect this experience of science in the outside world. This is time and again an attitude that teachers have to work to overcome, to demonstrate that *school* science is just as relevant and exciting as the science on offer outside school. They can do so through the careful choice of activities – activities that may or may not immediately be identifiable as scientific, activities for which the solution to the problem is not clear-cut, activities that harness imagination, excitement and interest. These types of activity ensure that the pupils are able to use their skills creatively and are not dependent on a certain level of scientific knowledge and/or understanding. The outcomes are necessarily uncertain, and it is this that appeals to a vast number of pupils, including the reluctant learners. The presentation, and enjoyment, of this type of activity is what aids the learner in developing positive attitudes towards science and science study in school, and promotes the importance of science for their everyday life. Developing such positive attitudes at an early stage will, in turn, develop positive attitudes in adults and add to their understanding of scientific information. Although very few of our children will go on to study science beyond school, or indeed work as scientists, positive attitudes towards science developed in school, alongside that outside school, may also lead to the development of a lifelong interest in science or an interest in working in areas that rely on science. The attitudes towards science we develop in all our learners are therefore very important for their study now and for their future.

What children think of science

At this point in the book I thought it would be interesting to ask a number of children what they think of science. I posed the question 'What is science?' to a number of pupils aged 7 to 10; Figure 2.1 shows some of their responses. These responses show that the children consider science to be about:

> I think science is something that you try to find out about. You can find science in an information book. You can find out what something does.

> I think science is to do with rocks and minerals, magnets, water and salt. Science is a subject about different things.

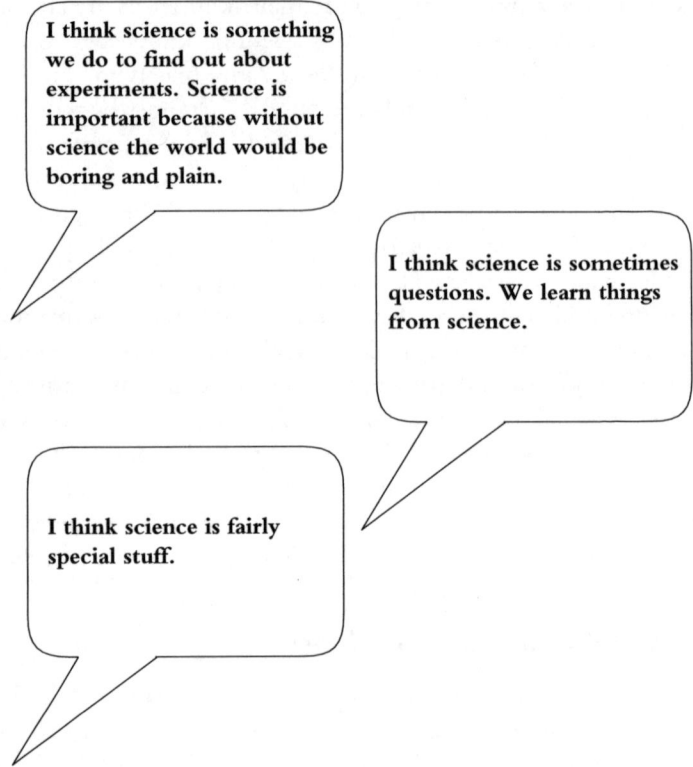

Figure 2.1 What is science?

- finding out;
- researching;
- natural phenomena;
- a variety of topics;
- experimenting;
- questioning;
- informing;
- special!

What a super list! These are the thoughts, attitudes and interests that we need to develop and maintain in all our pupils.

The science curriculum in England and Wales

It must be remembered that although science is a valuable subject to study, for all the reasons already suggested, its study is also an entitlement for pupils in England and Wales, with its own documentation setting out this entitlement. (An overview of the requirements of the documentation will be provided in Chapter 5.) The National Curriculum Order for Science (Qualifications and Curriculum Authority 1999a) and the Early Learning Goals (Qualifications and Curriculum Authority 1999b) are the documents that provide the outline for the science curriculum for the 3-years-plus age group. The Reception Profile at the end of the Foundation Stage provides assessment criteria for the early learning goals; assessments at the end of Key Stages 1, 2 and 3 are provided for within the National Curriculum Order for Science, after which GCSE syllabuses take over, although these continue to be based on the requirements of the National Curriculum Order for Science for Key Stage 4. Incidentally, there are changes planned to the science curriculum for Key Stage 4, to be implemented from September 2006: the key stage will cover ages 14–19 years and require all students to study science, but the current requirements (within the National Curriculum Order) will be replaced by a smaller, statutory core of requirements.

The documents do not prescribe a curriculum in terms of statutory activities to be carried out, but detail the knowledge, skills and breadth of experiences our pupils are to be provided with. It is this detail that enables us to formulate a science curriculum that is informative, developmental, relevant and interesting. The requirements include the need to encompass both the teaching *of* science, whereby pupils are involved in their own science work, and teaching *about* science, whereby pupils learn about scientific phenomena, theories and the work of scientists. Although a body of knowledge is prescribed by the documents, the style of study is not stated, and it is important to know that the documents set out a minimum requirement for the science curriculum, again allowing for a range of scientific activities to be carried out.

The basic requirements of the National Curriculum Order for

Science and the Early Learning Goals may be summed up as the study of:

- scientific knowledge – concepts and theories of science;
- the processes and methods of science – investigative skills;
- scientific enquiry – the application of investigative skills;
- scientific attitudes;
- the relationship between science and society.

Our youngest children, aged 3 to 5 years, use the Early Learning Goals (Qualifications and Curriculum Authority 1999b) as the basis for their science curriculum and yet science, as a named subject, does not exist. The richest source of ideas for their early science work is found under the heading 'Knowledge and understanding of the world', which encapsulates science, design and technology, history, geography, and information and communications technology (ICT). The actual requirements are shown in the box that follows.

Knowledge and understanding of the world

By the end of the Foundation Stage, children should be able to:

- investigate objects using their senses;
- find out about and identify some features of objects;
- look closely at similarities, differences, patterns and change;
- record findings;
- ask questions about why things happen and how things work;
- model investigative work;
- find out about the place they live in.

(QCA, 1999b)

At the age of 5, when children move from Reception to Year 1, the science curriculum is based firmly on the requirements of the National Curriculum Order for Science. The Order for Science has two main sections: the Programmes of Study and the

Attainment Targets. The Programmes of Study are used for planning the teaching and learning of science as they set out the knowledge, skills and understanding to be delivered to the pupil, whereas the Attainment Targets are used primarily for assessment purposes: they set out the knowledge, skills and understanding that pupils are expected to have *acquired* at different stages. In addition to their use in assessment, the Attainment Targets may also be used to aid the planning process, by indicating the level at which to pitch the teaching activities.

The Order acknowledges the need for both scientific process and content to be studied, both independently of each other and as interrelated strands. The strands are listed as:

- Scientific enquiry;
- Life processes and living things;
- Materials and their properties;
- Physical processes.

We will look at the requirements within these strands in more detail in Part 2 of this book.

Why some pupils find science difficult

This book is aimed at teachers of reluctant learners, but, if science can be so interesting, relevant and exciting, why do some pupils find studying the subject difficult or uninteresting? Unfortunately, there are many reasons! And yet, if we can identify why our pupils have negative attitudes or problems, this knowledge can be used to ensure that our science curriculum is appropriate and promotes more positive experiences for the learners. Some common reasons for the development of negative attitudes are the beliefs that:

- *school science is different from other science* – a myth perpetuated by interesting television programmes, websites and books compared to the perceptions of school science lessons;
- *science study is hard* – science is perceived as one of the more difficult subjects to study and understand;
- *science facts have to be remembered* – science is solely a body of knowledge to be learned and recalled;

- *school science isn't relevant to today's world* – the science studied is boring and out of date;
- *you have to get the right answer* – there is only one conclusion to be drawn;
- *you have to follow an experiment plan exactly* – if you don't follow the plan to the letter, you won't get the right answer;
- *the experiments are complex* – the plan is too hard to carry out;
- *science has an unpleasant smell* – school science involves unknown smelly chemicals;
- *science isn't for me* – science is for 'clever' learners;
- *science involves a lot of writing* – every investigation has to be written out in full, following a set format;
- *science involves a lot of reading* – reading of experiment instructions, or trawling through boring science books for information.

The list could go on; I'm sure you could add many more beliefs to the list. Our job is therefore to reverse these negative beliefs through the provision of a relevant, exciting and interesting curriculum. I have used this phrase many times already; indeed, the book is based on this requirement, and yet it is no mean feat to devise such a curriculum when today's pupils are subject to a range of experiences generated by numerous outside sources of information including television, video, the Internet and foreign travel. This plethora of ideas and developments may make the more traditional investigations in science seem old-fashioned and simplistic, and so, to state the case yet again, the identification of relevant ideas, problems to solve and investigations to carry out is indicated to enthuse all learners, including the more reluctant ones.

There are, of course, other reasons why particular learners may be reluctant to engage in science – reasons that have nothing to do with science as a subject. The reasons of this kind are complex and may not be easily identifiable in the pupil. Such reasons include:

- *lack of self-esteem* – the pupil believes he or she has nothing to offer;
- *a distorted self-image* – the pupil believes he or she can't achieve in any subject, so doesn't even try to achieve;
- *embarrassment about ability* – both high and low achievers may

be embarrassed about demonstrating their ability to their peers;

- *low ability in literacy skills* – the pupil is aware of his or her difficulties in reading, writing and/or speaking and listening, and so masks those difficulties by not engaging with the curriculum;
- *peer pressure* – the pupil's peer group do not value learning and so the pupil is pressured into not engaging with the learning;
- *behaviour problems* – the pupil may have difficulty maintaining positive behaviour (for a number of reasons), and this may impact on his or her engagement in science.

The effects of an interesting and relevant curriculum on pupils who are reluctant learners for any of the above reasons are touched on throughout the book.

3 The learning environment

When one is setting the scene for inspiring science, the learning environment is an important consideration. It is crucial to learning, as it is where the science curriculum truly comes alive, and so, although no two teaching rooms are the same in size and contents, it must be set out effectively, so as to stimulate learning for all pupils. The learning environment must be considered with respect to enhancing, supporting and encouraging the provision of exciting and relevant science activities. When thought of in this way, the learning environment is to be considered not only in terms of the layout of the furniture but also in terms of the organization of the available space, the use of display to inform and celebrate pupils' science work, and the provision of suitable equipment.

Furniture, layout and organization

Each teaching area will have its own available space and its own set of furniture that may or may not be movable. Little can be done by the teacher to alter these two facets! In addition, in the primary school, science will take place where all teaching takes place, whereas in the secondary school it will take place in a specific room. The key is therefore to make the best use of what you've got and to use it to set the scene for science. The furniture, layout and organization must all indicate that 'this lesson is going to be exciting'. The use of display (see p. 24) will bring the room truly alive, but it is the furniture and where it is placed that must be addressed first. The layout of the furniture is central to the activities that pupils will be engaged in, and the need for access to resources, for the pupils to walk around the room safely and for them to sit together in appropriate groupings are all to be considered. It is often trial and error with moving furniture that results in the best layout for your needs. Be bold and creative! Try different layouts and different combinations. Use any movable furniture to clearly define specific areas and general-purpose spaces in the teaching environment, with labels added to indicate the focus of each area. Two examples might be 'Science Bay' and 'messy area'. Be flexible: movable furniture is excellent for changing the layout of the environment if the activity or mix of activities requires a different arrangement.

This organization of the furniture is essential to the success of any lesson. Within my science lessons it is quite rare for pupils to engage in activities alone; it is much more usual for them to work in pairs or larger groups, and so the layout of the furniture must facilitate working in groups. I will consider further the advantages and disadvantages of paired or group work in Chapter 13 and 18, but the following are just a few of the advantages I believe working with peers brings to scientific activity:

- Pupils are able to share ideas.
- Paired and/or group work is less threatening for the less able or less confident pupil.
- Working with their peers enables pupils to challenge and extend their understanding.
- It promotes teamwork.
- It develops relationships between peers.
- Paired and/or group work develops tolerance: the accepting of differences of opinion, and dealing with them in a positive manner.
- It reduces the need for vast amounts of resources.
- Groups or pairs can be of mixed ability, with the more able helping the less able to access the activity, or of similar ability, to aid differentiation of the task by the teacher.
- The use of appropriate adult intervention in paired and/or group work will challenge the group further, and promote further discussion and investigation.
- Paired work provides the advantages of group work without the need to consider group dynamics or the equal sharing of tasks within the activity.

The layout and organization of the room must therefore facilitate pupils' working and interacting in this way; space must be provided for the pupils to communicate with each other without the intrusion of the conversations of others.

When you are considering the layout of the teaching environment, it is also important to remember your needs as the teacher. You will need:

- space to interact with the groups while keeping an overview of the whole class;
- to be able to move about freely, in order to observe, monitor and assess the pupils' learning;
- to establish your own rules for moving from one area to another;
- to stress the need for safe working practices, particularly with regard to the amount of movement allowed in the classroom.

Display

Displays are an integral and essential tool in teaching for many reasons, including the motivation of pupils. In science they may be used:

- to present scientific information – using labels, captions, statements, etc.;
- to set up an investigation to be accessed throughout the day – for example, a collection of objects to be categorized using a property of materials;
- to set up an investigation to be observed over time – for example, observing plants growing in different conditions;
- to provide a resource base for pupils – for example, a displayed range of equipment, glossary cards, information books;
- to celebrate the achievements and experiences of pupils – displaying a selection of pupils' work.

Each type of display ensures that the pupils are surrounded by science and relevant scientific information regardless of whether the room is used for all teaching or solely for science teaching. The benefits of display, particularly for reluctant learners, are manifold. I have begun to compile a list of the benefits that I believe effective displays bring to the science environment, but once again I am sure you could add many more benefits to the list.

- Displays can bring science alive.
- Interesting displays inspire scientific thought and enquiry.
- Displays can make science appear exciting and inspire pupils to get involved.
- Displays can provide a myriad of information that can be used by learners who are reluctant to engage with the teacher.
- Reluctant learners may be motivated to access scientific enquiry through the informality of a stimulus display (such as the display of objects to be categorized).
- Reluctant learners may be motivated by seeing their work carefully and attractively displayed.

It is essential that displays are attractive and well thought out, and use quality materials; displays that do not fit these criteria have the opposite effect to that which we intend. At best, inferior displays are ineffective, and at worst they are demotivating. Poorly presented displays help to perpetuate the myth that school science lessons are boring and dull, whereas effective displays are what bring a science teaching environment alive and stimulate an interest in the pupil towards continuing scientific study. With the requirement for teachers to put up displays having been removed from their contract of employment, it is essential that support staff and pupils are involved in planning and setting out displays, to foster an interest in the learners and to ensure both that a display is attractive and meaningful and that it will be used by the learners.

There are many considerations when one is planning displays; again it is for the teacher, support staff and children to be as creative as they wish. The layout of the room may dictate the site of a display, or the layout may be changed to accommodate the display. The display must be both visible and accessible, or there is little point in spending time on this aspect of the learning environment. Although it is advantageous to have all types of display in the teaching environment, it may not be possible to do so, owing to lack of space or the need for other subject displays. The overriding considerations are:

- Which of the five types of display will be most useful at the present time?
- What resources are needed to set up the display?

It must be remembered that effective display in the teaching environment involves the use of three-dimensional images and artefacts alongside two-dimensional ones, the provision of wall-mounted and surface displays, and, probably most important of all, the use of questions and captions on the displays. Questions and captions are what focus the learner on the content of the display; displays are ineffective if they do not encourage interaction by the observer, and so the questions and captions can be used to provide a starting point for this interaction and are what ensures that the display is used to full effect.

Equipment

The need for all pupils to have access to good-quality, relevant equipment and resources that promote the experience of an exciting and appropriate science curriculum simply cannot be overstated. The use of equipment and resources in science encourages pupils:

- to become familiar with a range of equipment;
- to appreciate that there may be more than one type of a piece of equipment;
- to become comfortable with using the equipment;
- to understand that sometimes there is a need for specialist equipment and sometimes a need for everyday equipment;
- to develop the ability to select the appropriate equipment to use;
- to develop an understanding of the need for care and safety when handling equipment and resources.

It can be appreciated that it is essential for pupils to use, handle and choose a range of equipment and resources in order to make their investigations and explorations worthwhile, and that much equipment can be provided at little cost. What is important to consider when creating an effective learning environment is what type of equipment is needed and how it will be stored and accessed by the pupils. As you might expect, a full list of equipment and resources is almost impossible to provide, although it goes without saying that a good selection of basic equipment is required to cover the range of activities you will present. This basic set of equipment can then be supplemented when a particular activity is delivered and the specific equipment required identified. In what follows, I provide what I would consider a good basic kit to include, listing the equipment under three headings:

1. specialist equipment;
2. everyday resources;
3. secondary resources.

The first two types are therefore primary resources for science and scientific enquiry, while the third list includes the sources of reference material you will want to provide. Once again, these lists are provided merely as starting points for you to consider and are certainly not essential requirements. I will also be providing more ideas for resources, particularly secondary resources, in Part Eight of the book.

Basic set of specialist equipment

- Weather equipment: anemometer, barometer, compass, hygrometer, rain gauge, weather board.
- Water equipment: aquarium.
- Viewing equipment: binoculars, range of magnifiers, range of sample boxes (with magnifying lids), microscopes, viewing boxes, range of lenses.
- Thermometers: a range of thermometers.
- Measuring equipment: callipers, height chart/measurer, metre sticks, tape-measures, a trundle wheel, measuring beakers, measuring cylinders, measuring jugs, measuring spoons, syringes, a range of stopwatches/clocks/timers, a range of scales and balances, metal masses, plastic masses, slotted masses and hangers.
- Flower equipment: a flower press, gardening tools, a propagator.
- Animal equipment: nets, pooters (a pooter is a plastic viewing box for collecting mini-beasts).

- The body: human torso, body models, e.g. ear, eye, brain, teeth, skeleton, stethoscope, X-rays.
- The earth: a globe, a pH meter/probe, quadrates, rocks and fossils, soils, a soil meter, sieves.
- Light: a light meter/sensor, coloured acetate sheets, colour paddles, mirrors, concave/convex mirrors, lenses, lens holders, a kaleidoscope, a light ray box, periscope, prisms, torches.
- Sound: musical instruments, plastic tubing, metal pipes, slinky (a large spring), a sound meter, tuning forks.
- Mixtures: droppers, litmus paper, pH paper, funnels, filter papers, a hob unit, metal rods, night lights, a pestle and mortar, stands, goggles, tongs.
- Electricity: batteries, battery holders, bells, bulbs, bulb holders, buzzers, crocodile clips, LEDs, motors, switches, chocolate block connectors, screwdrivers, wire, wire strippers.
- Magnetism: bar magnets, horseshoe magnets, polo magnets, fridge magnets, magnetic strip, magnetic tape, magnetic discs, magnetic marbles and wand, iron filings (encased), soft iron rods.
- Forces: force meters, rubber bands.

Ideas for a basic set of everyday resources
- Aluminium foil.
- Balloons and a balloon pump.
- A range of different-sized balls.
- A range of building equipment, e.g. bricks, tiles, slates, pebbles, sand, guttering.
- Marbles, beads.
- Bubble mixture and bubble blowers.
- A range of card and card pieces.
- Candles.
- Pegs, cotton reels.
- Compost, seeds, bulbs, plant pots, seed trays.
- Jam jars.
- A range of threads and strings.
- A range of spoons.
- Sponges.
- Springs.

- Straws.
- Corks, rubber bungs.
- Disposable cups.
- Disposable gloves.
- A range of wood – different sizes, shapes, types (including bark).
- Rubber bands.
- A range of paper.
- Paper clips, paper fasteners.
- A range of fabrics.
- A range of toys – magnetic, electrical, wind-up.
- A range of metal samples, nails.
- A range of plastic bags, plastic sheets, plastic containers, plastic bottles.
- Plasticine.

Basic range of secondary sources

- *Video and photographic resources*, e.g. video footage of the first man on the moon, photographs taken in space.
- *Specialist and non-specialist television programmes.* There are a number of television programmes shown each year that focus on aiding the teaching of the science curriculum. In addition to these, you could video programmes that are not aimed at teaching but demonstrate ideas in science. In doing this you will be using the interesting sources of information that pupils use outside school, thereby bridging the gap between *school* science and *other* science.
- *Non-fiction publications*, e.g. specialist science information books, encyclopedias and science dictionaries. In addition to these resources, newspapers and magazines often also have snippets of information the pupils may be interested in and may be able to use in their science study.
- *Fiction books.* There are many stories that can be used to convey science information and/or to inspire scientific investigations. I have noted some of these earlier in the book. Traditional stories are a particularly good resource for this inspiration, as are more modern short stories that involve the characters in using science skills or discovering science ideas for themselves.

- *Biographies of scientists and inventors*. These are an excellent source of information and inspiration in science. Many stories can be found in books and on the Internet.
- *Internet sites*. The world really is your oyster as far as the Internet and science is concerned! Later in the book I list my top ten sites for pupils (see Part Three) and teachers (see Part Eight), but the Internet changes rapidly and I find something new every time I search the web.

Storage of equipment

The storage of equipment, and its accessibility, are very important considerations, particularly for the reluctant learner who may be put off simply by either not having the correct equipment to hand or having to ask the teacher for a certain piece of equipment. Your school will most probably have a policy on the storage of equipment; it could require equipment to be housed in a central store or to be housed fully in individual classrooms. Alternatively, some equipment could be retained centrally and some – that which is used on a very regular basis – housed in the classroom. If equipment is housed fully in the classroom, it may be easier for pupils to access it, although there may be so much equipment that you have to put out a range for the pupils to select from, whereas if the equipment is stored centrally you will need to collect a range to display in the classroom, again for the pupils to select from. It is therefore not important to the learner *which* system is used but rather *how* it is used.

It goes without saying that the equipment presented for the pupil to use has to be in good condition, be safe to use, be age-appropriate for the pupils and be pupil-friendly. The equipment must also be up to date and relevant to the task. Only if these criteria for equipment are met will the equipment promote effective learning in science. However, having this range of good-quality equipment is useful only if it is accessible by the pupils. Wherever possible it should be presented in a way that encourages pupils to select their own equipment for the task, which is essential for developing their independence. One simple way to encourage this independence in selecting equipment is to label the storage of equipment in an appropriate, age-related way. Pupils can then be directed to refer to labels and/or pictures on storage containers to identify the equipment stored within, and then to select and handle some of the resources needed for their work. In this way, pupils will be encouraged to make informed choices about the most appropriate equipment and/or resources to use. Not only will the ability to make such choices lead to independence in scientific study, but also it will encourage the learners to take further responsibility for the learning environment, for keeping it tidy yet ready for scientific enquiry. I must state here that independence in choosing appropriate equipment is a skill to be developed over time; nursery–aged children cannot be expected to choose, from a selection of thermometers, the correct thermometer to use for a certain task! This is a skill to be taught and practised, and Figure 3.1 suggests how pupils may progress in choosing and using equipment in science.

(a)

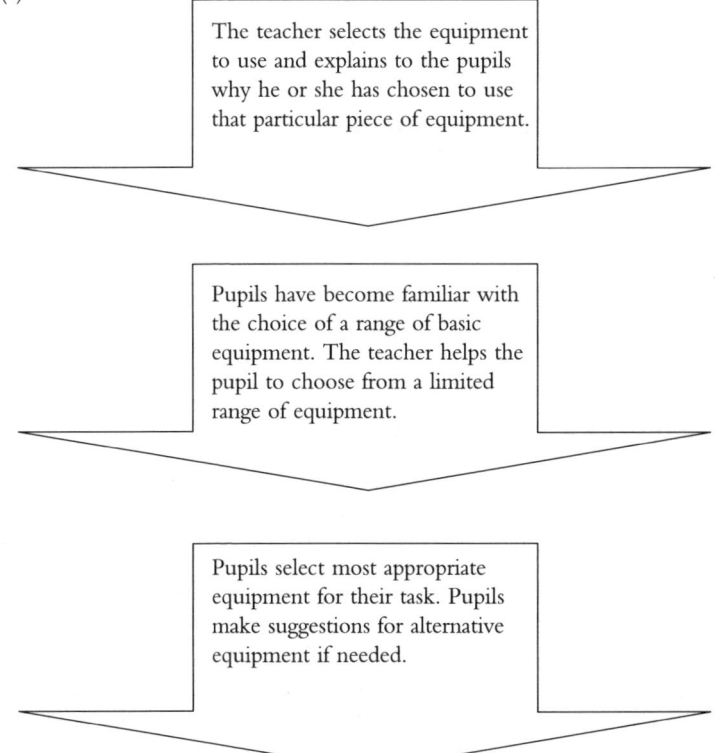

The teacher selects the equipment to use and explains to the pupils why he or she has chosen to use that particular piece of equipment.

Pupils have become familiar with the choice of a range of basic equipment. The teacher helps the pupil to choose from a limited range of equipment.

Pupils select most appropriate equipment for their task. Pupils make suggestions for alternative equipment if needed.

(b)

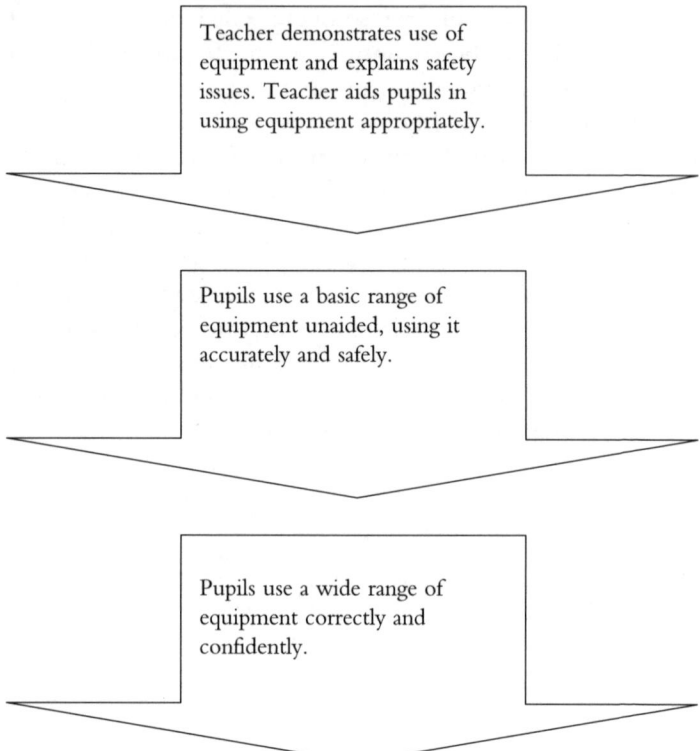

Teacher demonstrates use of equipment and explains safety issues. Teacher aids pupils in using equipment appropriately.

Pupils use a basic range of equipment unaided, using it accurately and safely.

Pupils use a wide range of equipment correctly and confidently.

Figure 3.1 Suggested progressions in (a) choosing and (b) using equipment in science

The outdoor environment

Another very important resource in science, and an additional learning environment, is the space beyond the nursery or classroom. This includes the immediate area outside the classroom, the school grounds and further afield – that is, visits into, and beyond, the community. These resources are essential to maintaining the interest of reluctant learners and for providing the links between school science study and the outside world. The immediate outdoor environment and that within the school grounds are particularly rich resources for scientific work, from the provision of a convenient setting for a potentially 'messy' activities, such as investigations into floating and sinking, and the facility to work on a large scale, such as the investigating of bubbles using large and small bubble wands, or observing living things in their natural environment through the study of plants in the school garden. This use of the immediate environment is particularly motivating for the reluctant learner as it encourages investigations that are meaningful and real, and literally removes the boundaries of the classroom. The only limitation to its use is the teacher's imagination! Many investigations can be taken outside, which brings science to *life* for many learners. The opportunity to study the formation of shadows by the sun through observing how a shadow of a stick changes throughout the day is much more motivating for the learner than using a book or CD-ROM for the necessary information, as is the opportunity for studying the properties of different rocks and soils. The youngest pupils, those in the Foundation stage of learning, use the outdoors area as a necessary part of their learning environment, building on their knowledge and understandings of the world through interacting with living things (including people) and objects in the natural environment, thus developing the necessary knowledge of the world they live in; and these experiences are equally valuable for older reluctant learners.

Using environments beyond school

The learning environment must therefore include all teaching areas: the classroom; areas within school used for science study, such as the library; an area between classrooms, the corridor, areas immediately outside the classroom; the school grounds; and areas beyond the school gates. All can provide real opportunities to link school experiences with life in school and in the wider world. The use of environments beyond school is particularly motivating for all learners, as such environments can introduce pupils to experiences they could not have inside the classroom, such as observing the seas in motion or larger animals in a natural habitat. The careful use of environments beyond the school can therefore make a significant contribution to the development of pupils' scientific knowledge and understanding, and offer the much-needed insight into the use of science in everyday life.

There are many, many environments that may be used as part of the science curriculum, from science centres and museums to a walk in the local park to observe forces in action. As with anything in teaching, preparation is the key. A pre-visit is essential. If *you* don't enjoy the experience and enthuse about it, then the reluctant learner will hardly be inspired by the experience! The first considerations are the appropriateness of the visit, its nature and purpose, and the health and safety implications. Younger pupils benefit from planned visits close to the nursery or school, where they are starting from the familiar, while older pupils are better able to cope with, and often more motivated by, a visit further afield that involves a longer journey. Local visits do, however, provide the opportunity to establish your expectations about behaviour and how to deal with other adults, and so may be appropriate for older learners and the more reluctant learners before venturing further afield.

Pre-visits are essential for:

- *Judging the value of the visit* – in terms of the learning experiences it can provide.
- *Judging the suitability of the visit* – in terms of the venue being age-appropriate, the height of displays, the provision of written (and pictorial) information, labels and captions, etc.
- *Deciding where the learning to take place on the visit fits into the science topic being studied in school.* Will the visit be used to launch the topic or to provide extra information during the topic, or will it take place at the end of the topic to demonstrate the use of the science learned in school in a real-life setting?
- *Identifying the work needed in school* – in preparation for the visit and following the visit. The pupils may need to research information in preparation for the visit, they may need a certain level of understanding before the visit in order to access the learning on the visit, or they may benefit from generating a list of questions to be answered during the visit. Following the visit, the pupils may be inspired to research information and/or to carry out investigations, and you will need to be able to help them do so. Incidentally, I think there is nothing more off-putting for pupils than a request to write about their visit; it is much more appropriate to use the

visit to generate meaningful study through research and/or further investigation.

- *Identifying how much of the visit venue will be used.* Will the visit use the whole site or only part of it? Are there learning opportunities to be found inside the venue and outside?
- *Considering the use of time on the visit.* How much time is needed for the journey to and from the venue and how long will the pupils spend in and around the venue?
- *Identifying the basic facilities provided* – the ease of the travel arrangements, the ease of booking into the visit venue, the availability of toilets, a classroom area, storage for coats and bags, an area for eating lunch, etc.
- *Identifying the involvement of other adults.* Other adults will be needed on the visit to supervise the pupils. (Your local education authority will have guidelines on the ratio of adults to pupils on visits.) You will need to identify who these adults will be and whether they can contribute to the pupils' learning experiences. There may be parents of pupils, governors of the school or support staff who are experts on the area you are visiting or studying and can add much-needed information regarding the visit. The venue may supply an education officer or guide, or you may be able to pay extra to have one provided.
- *Identify the risk assessment needed.* Risk assessments are needed when taking pupils on visits. They must set out clearly any potential dangers facing the pupils, and the measures to be taken to avoid the dangers, in order to ensure the pupils' safety.

There is thus quite a lot to think about when planning a visit, and yet the effort is well worthwhile, as a well-planned, well-thought-out visit can inspire learning before, during and after the visit. The work you put into this aspect of the science curriculum is therefore an excellent investment.

Health and safety

One final consideration when using the whole of the learning environment, both inside the classroom and beyond, is the teacher's legal duty to provide an effective and safe learning environment where pupils can feel secure and confident, and in which they can operate safely and purposefully. It is unrealistic to seek to ensure that a classroom can be totally risk free, just as the home can never be risk free, but pupils' health and safety must be addressed in line with the Health and Safety at Work Act 1974. Teachers must also be mindful of their common-law duty of care to act *in loco parentis*, and so it is essential that teachers are knowledgeable about both the likely actions of their pupils in a given situation and the risks associated with science activity. The following is a checklist of basic guidelines for the teacher for ensuring the health and safety of pupils in science.

- Carry out a risk assessment before an activity takes place, identifying potential safety issues.
- Try out the activity before presenting it to the pupil.
- Identify activities that require careful supervision and prepare for this level of supervision.
- Identify activities that require the restricted use of resources by the pupils.
- Consider safer alternative activities and/or approaches to the activity.
- Ensure that the learning environment is properly prepared before the activity takes place and is adequately cleaned following the activity.
- Consult the ASE publication *Be Safe!* (Association for Science Education 2001).

The teacher is expected to have a certain degree of foresight in the learning environment, and the failure to prevent injury or harm to a pupil when the dangers could be reasonably have been foreseen constitutes negligence. However, the risk of a pupil falling over, trapping a finger or generally mishandling equipment is a possibility in most classrooms, and so teachers must build into their teaching the skills of personal risk avoidance, risk awareness and risk management techniques. I have provided in Figure 3.2 a model for the expected progression in the safe use of equipment that is essential for pupils to develop over time.

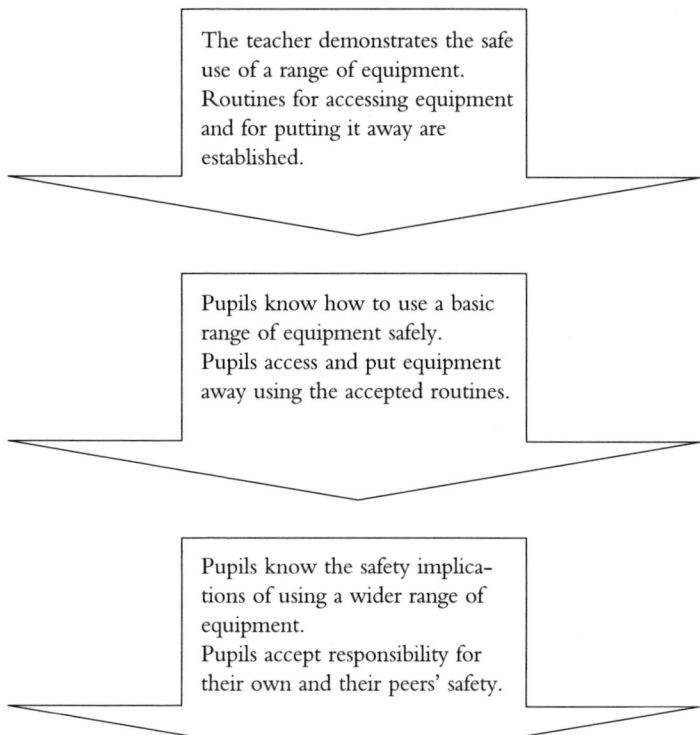

Figure 3.2 Expected progression in the safe use of equipment

Part Two

Getting Started

4 Getting motivated

Part One of the book set the scene for the study of science and introduced some ideas for getting exciting, relevant and inspiring science established within the classroom. Later in this part of the book I will look in more detail at the documentation that accompanies the science curriculum, and the science curriculum that the documentation indicates, but it is important to note that the science you present to your pupils need not be constrained by the requirements of this documentation. The documentation sets out a *minimum* requirement only, and so further study is more than acceptable. It also sets out simply *what* is to be learned and not *how* it is to be learned (although it does offer suggestions), and so it is the skill of the teacher in interpreting the documentation that is central to providing a relevant, interesting and inspiring curriculum that motivates all learners within the classroom.

The documentation is therefore to be used to provide the basis for a range of activities that, first, engage the pupils in developing the use of scientific skills, developing their scientific knowledge, developing attitudes to self and environment, and developing attitudes to science; and second, require them to work with and discuss their learning with others. It is supplemented by other relevant activities that support learners in their learning in science. This part of the book will provide you with some ideas for using the documentation, for supplementing it and for making your science teaching interesting, exciting and relevant. As with all the ideas I am presenting in the book, I hope you will use them merely as starting points for getting motivated, as I do believe the best ideas for your teaching, and your pupils' learning, are those that you develop yourself.

Ten minutes to spare?

A few years ago, when the literacy and numeracy strategies came into primary schools, an LEA adviser suggested that scientific activities could be used to fill any of the ten-minute slots that now sometimes occur in the daily timetable. I began to think about this and tried to come up with a number of ideas for activities to fill these slots that would provide meaningful learning in science, through either the introduction or the consolidation of science ideas, and I generated quite a list. I have listed my 'top ten' below, with explanations where needed and the possible learning opportunities they provide.

1. 'I'm thinking of . . .' twenty questions to identify an object

For example:

Teacher, or Pupil 1: I'm thinking of a fruit.
   Pupil 2: Is it spherical?
Teacher, or Pupil 1: No.
   Pupil 3: Does it have a stone inside?
Teacher, or Pupil 1: Yes.
   Pupil 4: Is it a large fruit?
Teacher, or Pupil 1: No.
   Pupil 5: Is it a cherry?
Teacher, or Pupil 1: Yes.

This activity involves the pupils in using known properties to identify an object. It can be used with many groups of objects.

2. Playing 'Guess the Person'

All pupils stand up. The teacher (or another pupil) chooses a pupil and then invites the pupils to start to ask questions to identify the pupil he or she is thinking of.

Question: Is this person wearing black?
Answer: Yes.

Anyone not wearing black then sits down.

Question: Is this person wearing trainers?
Answer: No.

All pupils wearing trainers sit down. (The game continues until only one pupil is left standing.)

This activity involves the pupils in using the skill of observation, which is an important skill to develop in science. It also uses questions to separate a group of objects (people!) into two groups, the forerunner of being able to devise and use keys for grouping objects.

3. Making a prediction
Which will fall to floor first – a flat piece of paper or a screwed up one? This can be easily tested in seconds, and the pupils discuss the result, in pairs, groups or as a whole class.

This activity can be used to demonstrate how useful predictions can be, how and why predictions vary, and how previous knowledge can be used when making a prediction. It can be used to discuss the science involved in what happened or to demonstrate how results can be matched to the prediction made.

4. Testing pulls using a force meter
Provide force meters to use when pulling classroom objects, such as a drawer or a pencil case. This activity can be used to introduce the pupils to the use of equipment, to how the equipment is to be used safely, to the notion of forces, to the measurement of forces and/or to the comparison of the size of force needed for different objects.

5. Timing an event accurately
Have pupils use a stopwatch to time a simple event, such as a piece of paper falling to ground. The usefulness of this activity is similar to that of activity 4: it teaches pupils how to use the equipment and may be used to compare different types of timing device and to identify the most appropriate for the task.

6. My healthy meal
Pupils discuss in groups the theme 'today's healthy meal is . . .' and then make a presentation to the class.

7. The dictionary game
The teacher gives the pupils a science word to find in the dictionary and give a definition to the class. This could be a

question for older pupils to find the answer to – for example, what is the speed of light?

This can be a short, simple activity that provides information for use later in the classroom, that introduces pupils to specific vocabulary in science, or that develops the pupils' confidence in sharing their ideas verbally within a group or the whole class.

8. Today's scientist is ...
Read the story of a scientist to the class.

I'm sure you are beginning to appreciate how important I think the stories of scientists are to the science curriculum! The story may be used simply as the appreciation of how a scientist lived and worked. Alternatively, an issue the story raises may be discussed, or the work the scientist did and its relevance to the pupils may be considered.

9. Invent a mnemonic
The pupils are challenged to produce an original mnemonic – for example, for the order of the planets, or the life process. This activity gets pupils talking about science facts and using their knowledge of words. It can be used to promote the learning of facts or to introduce the facts, but the learning is not dry and boring but is fun and active.

10. 'Today's list is ...'
Pupils are challenged to produce the longest list in the time available – for example, the names of the human bones, types of bird, or different habitats. This enables pupils to work together – in pairs, groups or the whole class – to share their knowledge and ideas. Again it is a fun way for them to use their knowledge, and it ensures that all learners are included, regardless of their ability to memorize facts.

Most of the activities need little or no setting up and require no formal recording by the pupils. The benefits of these types of activity are that they are short, snappy, fun and not threatening. Particularly for the reluctant learner, they develop and maintain motivation, and have often inspired my pupils to suggest their own ten-minute activities.

Paper planes, football shirts and ice-lollies

This section describes three of my favourite activities, activities that have never yet failed to inspire pupils!

Paper planes

I'm sure most children have made paper planes at some time, and not only to be allowed to make them in the classroom, but to be *asked* to make them appears to some pupils to border on being allowed to be naughty in the classroom! I usually start the lesson by demonstrating how I make a simple paper plane and showing them how it flies. I then challenge the pupils to make their own. At this point they may choose to use my design or, more often, to use a design of their own.

After encouraging the pupils to test and modify their planes, I show them how adding weight, using paper clips, affects the flight of my plane. I then ask them what they think the effects of using a different paper to make my plane would be. This leads on to a discussion of *variables* and *fair testing* and to the pupils designing their own investigation using their own planes.

I liken the success of this lesson, and other successful lessons, to that of a good story! This metaphor does help me to plan effective science lessons and may be an effective model for you to work from. The metaphor works because a good story has to have the following:

- *A good, clear beginning.* For this activity, it is the demonstration of making and flying my plane.
- *A gripping middle.* In this activity, the pupils' making and flying their own planes successfully and then planning and carrying out their own investigations are particularly exciting parts of the lesson!
- *A good ending.* The lesson ends with a purpose: the demonstration of their planes, describing their investigation and their results.
- *An exciting plot.* The *plot* here is the development of a super-plane.

Viewed in this way, it can be appreciated that the clear beginning, to both a good story and a good lesson, requires a well-planned introduction to the activity. The gripping middle of the lesson is the active part the pupils will be engaged in, and the good ending is where the pupils are able to describe their work and reflect on their learning. The plot of any story is essential to its success, and the same is true of a good lesson, and so the development of the super-plane is what engages the children so successfully in this activity.

Football shirts

A major requirement of the science curriculum is the use of keys for assigning plants and animals to groups and for the grouping of materials using the properties of materials. The ability to use a key is quite a complex skill that needs to be taught over time, beginning with simply separating a group of objects or pictures into two groups following a question to be asked, such as 'Has it got two legs?' For the reluctant learner, this is hardly inspiring! In order to develop the formulation and use of keys, I look for other objects to inspire pupils and have found football shirts and cartoon characters to be among the most motivating. You do need to get to know your pupils and their interests and then use these interests as a context for this activity.

When using football shirts as a context, I ask the pupils to draw four or six football shirts along the top of a sheet of paper and then begin to ask questions to separate them into two groups, such as 'Does the shirt have a round neck?' The pupils carry on until the key is formed and then have it *checked* by another pupil. The same instructions are used for cartoon characters or whatever objects the pupils are focusing on.

Through this activity the pupils are learning to form and use keys and develop their observational skills without the constraint of using traditional scientific objects or materials to group. The presentation of a more scientifically based key is later introduced and accepted, as the pupils already have the skills needed to use keys.

Ice-lollies

There is an activity developed by a colleague of mine that she has found successful with a number of groups of pupils. When covering the requirement in the National Curriculum for pupils to know that some materials are better thermal insulators than others, she brings into school a box of ice-lollies and explains to the class that she's brought them for her breaks this week but the freezer in the staffroom has broken down over the weekend. What should she do? She's willing to share them with the staff, but they need to be kept frozen until afternoon break time.

This introduction follows work carried out into the properties of different materials, and soon the pupils begin to suggest wrapping the lollies in different materials to keep them frozen. Of course, my colleague doesn't know which material to choose and asks the pupils to help her to choose. The lollies are then wrapped in the different materials suggested by the pupils and are observed at different times during the day.

This is a very good activity because it poses a real-life problem for the pupils to solve. It requires the pupils to use previous knowledge, to set up a fair test and to carry out accurate observations. It is certainly an inspiring way of teaching them about thermal insulation.

Balloons

Children of all ages love balloons and are fascinated by their properties. Balloons can be used to generate much discussion about air, floating and gravity, together with the properties of rubber or the material the balloon is made of. Another successful activity I have used has been based on a balloon and how we could stop it floating to the very high ceiling in the classroom. The inspiration for this activity came from a question at the end of the Key Stage 2 SATs test about the effects of adding paper clips to a helium balloon and why doing so prevented the balloon from rising.

I brought into school a 'Happy Birthday' balloon filled with helium and asked the pupils why they thought I had to hold on to it all the time. This led on to a discussion of why the balloon was floating and the effects of the gas within the balloon, gravity and air resistance. We moved on to the concept of weight and began changing the weight of the balloon, using paper clips. The pupils predicted how many paper clips would be needed to keep the balloon at a level I could reach, and we tested it out together.

This session was an excellent starting point for the pupils to explore their own understanding of the relationship between gravity, weight and air resistance, and led on to the children wanting to investigate further but this time using parachutes.

Into the garden

I stressed in Chapter 3 the advantages of extending the learning environment using spaces outside the classroom and into the school grounds. The outside environment is a rich source of information about plants, animals and habitats, and can be inspirational for the most reluctant of learners. There are many investigations and activities that can be carried out, including:

- *A mini-beast hunt.* How many species of mini-beast can the groups see and photograph using a digital camera?
- *A flower parade.* How many different species of flower grow in the school garden?
- *A materials trail.* How many different materials can be found outside the school building?
- *How does your garden grow?* Where do plants and flowers grow? What are the conditions like where they grow?

These, and many more, activities can lead on to further investigations in the classroom and may be used to generate research activities to identify the animals photographed, the plants observed, the materials found, the conditions for growth for plants and the features of the habitats the animals were located in.

5 The documentation

The main documentation for devising the science curriculum consists of the National Curriculum Order for Science (Qualifications and Curriculum Authority 1999a) and the Early Learning Goals within the area of study 'Knowledge and understanding of the world' for the Foundation Stage of learning (Qualifications and Curriculum Authority 1999b). I have already stated that these documents set out a minimum entitlement for your pupils, and so the science you deliver need not be constrained by them and does not need to be found only within these documents. However, the National Curriculum is a *statutory* document that details the knowledge, skills and understandings that children are to be taught within different key stages; it also determines how the performance of children will be assessed and reported, and so it is an extremely important document to get to know and interpret in practice. The Early Learning Goals establish a range of expectations for most children to reach by the end of the Foundation Stage, albeit not a statutory curriculum for our pre-5 years children but an essential basis for planning within the Foundation Stage of learning. In addition to these two documents, the Qualifications and Curriculum Authority has produced exemplar schemes of work for science that provide numerous ideas for activities for pupils of all ages. In this chapter I intend to look in more detail at the requirements of the science curriculum as indicated by the Early Learning Goals for 'Knowledge and understanding of the world' and the four strands of the National Curriculum Order for Science.

Using the Early Learning Goals

The Foundation Stage was introduced as a separate phase of education for children aged 3 to 5 years in September 2000. The requirements for this stage of learning are set out in the document *Curriculum Guidance for the Foundation Stage* (Qualifications and Curriculum Authority 2000). Within this document, six areas of learning are listed:

- Personal, social and emotional development;
- Communication, language and literacy;
- Mathematical development;
- Knowledge and understanding of the world;
- Physical development;
- Creative development.

It is within each area of learning that the Early Learning Goals are detailed. The most useful area of learning for practitioners devising a science curriculum for this age group is the area of learning 'Knowledge and understanding of the world'; this area also encompasses technology, history, geography, and ICT. The guidance for this area requires children to be engaged in activities that encourage:

- interest;
- curiosity;
- exploration;
- observation;
- problem solving;
- prediction;
- critical thinking;
- decision making;
- discussion;
- communication;
- recording findings;
- gathering information from a range of sources;
- development of skills, knowledge and attitudes.

I would list these as requirements for a science curriculum for pupils of any age! Indeed, the ideas presented throughout this book are based on the development of these skills, knowledge, understandings and attitudes. The requirements of the curriculum for the Foundation Stage, the ideals they are based upon and the documentation for this age group certainly support the need for exciting, relevant and inspiring work in science for all pupils, not solely the reluctant learners. The documentation suggests that relevant activities for the science curriculum include activities that involve:

- the use of a range of equipment, including magnifiers, gardening tools, etc.;
- encountering animals, people, plants and objects, in natural environments and in real-life situations;
- first-hand experience – for example, observing small vehicles travelling down slopes of different inclinations;
- using and handling materials, such as wet and dry sand, soils, pebbles, etc.

Again these mirror the needs of a relevant science curriculum for all ages.

The Early Learning Goals are what the majority of children at the end of the Foundation Stage are expected to achieve and, although they are quite brief, they do indicate that a range of explorations and investigations will have taken place during the Foundation Stage in order for the goals to be met. Within the documentation, stepping stones to the Early Learning Goals are detailed that set out the knowledge, skills, understanding and attitudes that children need to develop in order to achieve these goals, together with examples of pupils' achievements to aid practitioners in identifying milestones in the pupils' learning and indicating the learning yet to be developed. The Early Learning Goals for 'Knowledge and understanding of the world' that are related to science are listed below.

- Investigate objects and materials by using all of their senses as appropriate.
- Find out about, and identify, some features of living things, objects and events they observe.
- Look closely at similarities, differences, patterns and change.
- Ask questions about why things happen and how things work.
- Observe, find out about and identify features in the place they live and the natural world.
- Find out about their environment.

The four strands of the National Curriculum Order for Science

Within the National Curriculum Order for Science, the requirements are set out under four strands:

- Scientific enquiry (Sc1);
- Life processes and living things (Sc2);
- Materials and their properties (Sc3);
- Physical processes (Sc4).

Scientific enquiry, often referred to as science 1 (Sc1), covers the teaching of scientific skills and investigative work; the other three strands together cover the content of science prescribed by the document. For the purposes of this book, I have labelled 'Scientific enquiry' as *finding out*, as it covers the scientific skills, interpretations, attitudes and language required at different ages and stages, together with the knowledge of scientists and their work and the relevance of science to everyday life. The other three strands will be considered together under the heading *the important bits*. It is the investigative *finding out* strand of science that I find particularly interesting personally and I find is very motivating for reluctant learners, but an understanding of basic scientific concepts is also vital for the curriculum to be truly a scientific one. Also, not all science can be learned through investigation or observation, and so research by the pupils, using secondary sources of information, is a necessary part of the science curriculum. Where investigation and observation are used, it is important that pupils are able to discuss their work, to interpret their results and to justify their findings. School science must therefore be based on interplay between content delivery and enquiry, the learning and understanding of theories, and the learning and use of the skills that have led scientists to form those theories, and for pupils to make their own discoveries. Where investigation is appropriate, it is the role of the teacher to ensure that the pupil has the opportunity to reflect fully on the activity.

Science 1: finding out

The scientific enquiry strand of the National Curriculum Order for Science (Qualifications and Curriculum Authority 1999a) sets out the skills to be acquired for carrying out investigations and explorations in science. The skills listed include predicting, observing, measuring, recording, checking results, drawing conclusions and communicating findings. Although the skills need to be developed over time, it is inappropriate, and not particularly motivating, to teach them without a relevant context. The ideas given at the beginning of this part of the book – the ideas for getting started in science – demonstrated how to use a real-life context for pupils to make use of their scientific enquiry skills: preventing ice-lollies from melting, and extending or improving the flight of a paper plane. These are the types of scenario that will engage reluctant learners; they rely on relevant contexts for the pupils rather than on replicating a given investigation, and mirror the use of the skills by scientists in the *real world*. For scientists, the skills are necessary to determine the establishment of new theories, through investigation into ideas and phenomena and the interpretation of observations and results, and although it is most unlikely that new theories in science will arise from a school-based exploration, the pupils use scientific skills in the same way. The skills are necessary for the pupils' investigations, leading to knowledge that will provide the solution to the problem they are posed. This use of scientific skills consequently develops the pupils' knowledge and understanding of the skills and their usage, develops positive attitudes towards science and develops both an understanding and empathy for the way in which scientists work.

It can be appreciated that in order to devise suitable activities for pupils to develop their knowledge and understanding of the skills required for investigative work, it is most important that the teacher is him or herself able to identify the skills that need to be practised and developed. Using stories such as Winnie-the-Pooh and Cinderella (see Chapter 1) will help teachers to identify these skills, as will the following simple activity I have used with teachers during a training day.

'Stand up, sit down'

In pairs, the teachers labelled themselves Partner A and Partner B. I then explained the task: Partner A was to find out how many times Partner B could stand up and sit down in 1 minute, and to plan and carry out his or her investigation. Following this part of the investigation we drew up a list of skills used:

- considering different ways to find out the answer to a question;
- thinking about what might happen and why;
- making a prediction – although it was unlikely that the prediction could be based on any previous knowledge;
- trying ideas out – for example, whether to start in a standing position or a knees bent position, what and how to count, etc;
- making simple choices: how to carry out the investigation, what observations and measurements to make, etc.;
- identifying the equipment to be used;
- using simple equipment appropriately;
- taking action to control risks – to prevent Partner B from falling;
- making systematic observations and measurements;
- recording observations;
- drawing conclusions from the observations made;
- communicating the findings in an appropriate and systematic manner.

Quite a number of skills needed for such a simple activity! Some of the participants also checked their observations by repeating them, reviewed how they had worked, and described the significance and limitations of their investigation.

The next part of the activity was for Partner B to find out how many times Partner A could stand up and sit down in 1 minute, to plan and carry out the investigation and again identify the skills used. Following this part of the activity, we listed the use of the following skills in addition to those listed above:

- making a prediction based on previous knowledge, using the results of Partner A;
- making the test fair: using a chair of the same height, and the same starting position for both partners;
- making comparisons and identifying simple patterns or

associations in observations and measurements – by comparing the results of Partner A and Partner B;

- comparing the results and conclusions with predictions made;
- using scientific knowledge and understanding to explain observations and conclusions – for example, Partner A completed more as he was younger than Partner B.

This is an excellent activity for adults to use to help them in identifying a range of scientific skills; it is also excellent for use with pupils as they find it quite fun to carry out, and it often leads to their suggesting further investigations.

Reflecting and discussing

The development of pupils' knowledge and understanding of the skills of scientific enquiry is important:

- for developing positive attitudes towards science and scientific discovery;
- for developing an understanding and empathy for the way in which scientists work;
- to enable the pupils to investigate ideas for themselves.

It is therefore important not only for the teacher to be able to identify the skills used in science, as above, but also for the pupils themselves to be able to identify them, to be able to use them appropriately *and* to appreciate why they are important and how they develop our understanding in science. It is also vital that scientific enquiry involves the reflection and discussion between peers and between pupils and adults that enable the pupils to clarify their ideas and thinking, and so pupils must be taught that this too is a skill to be developed. The acquisition of this skill ensures that the pupils understand how the other skills of scientific enquiry lead to discoveries, whereas reflection and discussion between peers is what leads to the discoveries being accepted as true. Again this may be reinforced through the use of the stories of scientists. The story of Christian Doppler illustrates this importance of reflection and discussion well.

Christian Doppler was born in Salzburg in Austria in 1803 and died in 1853. His family were stonemasons and it was expected that he would take up the trade and join the family firm. This was not to be. Christian began studying maths in Vienna in 1822 and in 1829 became an assistant to a professor of maths and mechanics at the University of Vienna. He moved around over the next few years, working as a bookkeeper, a schoolteacher and a professor of maths at various institutions, and in 1850 was appointed the first director of the new Institute of Physics at Vienna University.

Although he had specialized in maths, Christian's true potential was realized in physics. He wrote many papers about his investigations into light and sound, and one particular scientist was impressed by what Christian wrote: Bernard Bolzano, a Czech mathematician. Bolzano wrote to many other scientists to urge them to read about Christian's work. Christian himself consulted the work of others, including the work of Augustin Fresnel, a French scientist, and used the findings to assist in his own investigations. Christian's first interpretations of his findings were flawed but were discussed within the scientific community and developed by Christian. His discoveries became accepted as the Doppler effect. (I find the Doppler effect to be quite a complex theory about sound waves, but is most easily explained by saying that what you hear depends upon whether you, or the source of sound, are moving or not!)

The story illustrates how the skills of reflection and discussion helped to shape Christian's ideas resulting from his investigations; his investigations were not enough on their own to lead to new theories. This story is one of many that can illustrate how scientific knowledge is arrived at and enable pupils to develop empathy with scientists and their work. This empathy in turn leads to an understanding of why scientific enquiry is important to us in everyday life, as it has led to our understanding of how things work and to many technological advances. The Christian Doppler story also clearly demonstrates why pupils need to use the skills of reflection and discussion in their explorations and investigations.

Using the skills

The pupils' use of scientific skills to carry out their own explorations and investigations, with no right or wrong answers to be arrived at, is what often appeals to the reluctant learner. Most pupils, even the most reluctant of learners, are naturally curious, and it is this curiosity that teachers need to capitalize on to motivate their pupils in science and scientific enquiry. It is therefore time well spent to identify pupils' interests and use these as starting points for science. It is through these personal enquiries that pupils will become engaged in the science curriculum, as they can identify a purpose for their work and gain the necessary experience of examining and questioning evidence.

Initially pupils use their current knowledge and understanding to interpret the results of their investigations; increasing maturity, experience and appropriate intervention by the teacher will lead on to pupils being able to understand, explain and interpret their findings in a more scientifically accepted approach. The ultimate goal is for pupils to accept that results and observations can be interpreted differently and that these different interpretations are valid and will lead on to a shared interpretation that can be accepted as *true*. This progression in developing the knowledge, understanding and use of skills is important for all pupils, to enable their understanding of science as a whole to develop, and is the key for teaching scientific enquiry.

The starting point for pupils' own investigations has to be the context for the investigation, yet I have found that one of the hardest skills for pupils to acquire is that of generating a question to be investigated. The use of stories, poems and problems to solve (as described throughout the book) can all promote ideas for investigation, and in Chapter 6 I will describe an activity I have used many times to aid pupils in identifying a question to investigate. However, the teaching of the skills for enquiry cannot be put on hold until pupils are able to suggest their own investigations. Indeed, the skills are needed *before* the pupils suggest their own investigations, in order for them to carry out their own explorations effectively. A model for the progression of skills acquisition in science is shown in Figure 5.1.

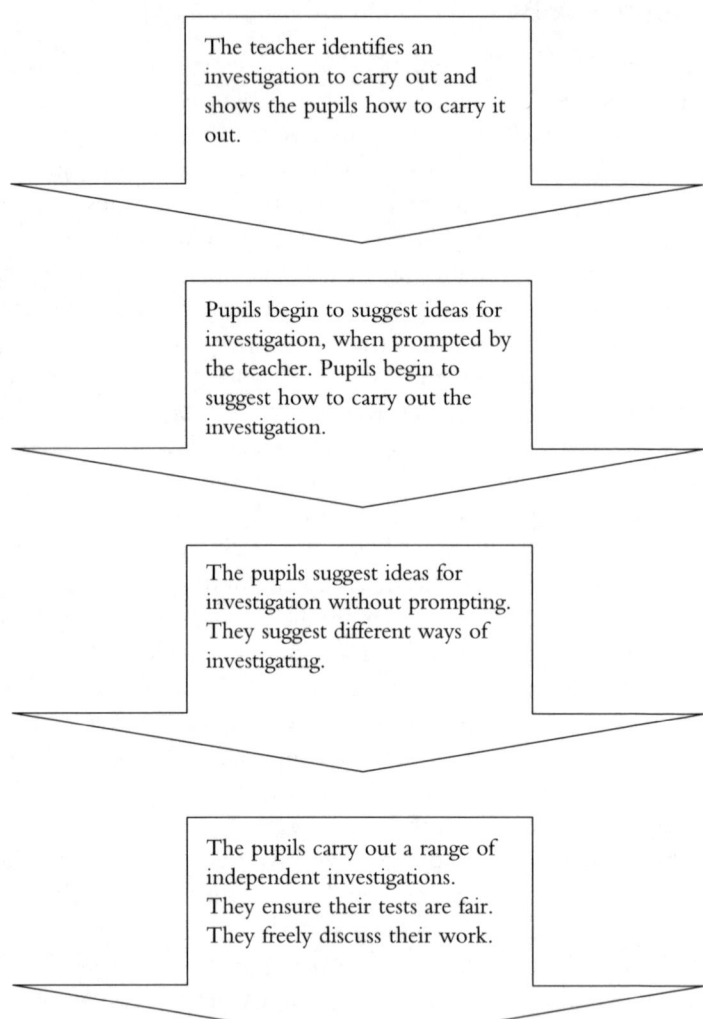

The teacher identifies an investigation to carry out and shows the pupils how to carry it out.

Pupils begin to suggest ideas for investigation, when prompted by the teacher. Pupils begin to suggest how to carry out the investigation.

The pupils suggest ideas for investigation without prompting. They suggest different ways of investigating.

The pupils carry out a range of independent investigations. They ensure their tests are fair. They freely discuss their work.

Figure 5.1 Progression of skills

The value of scientific enquiry

The value of scientific enquiry simply cannot be overstated. It is a means of motivating and stimulating pupils' interest in science and the science curriculum. It aids pupils in finding answers to questions about science and about scientists and their work from a range of sources, while drawing heavily on investigative skills, both skills unique to science and skills that are not necessarily unique to science. The skills not unique to science include the ability to cooperate, to share ideas and information, to use all the senses, to apply existing knowledge, to ask questions and to deploy research skills, including the use of ICT. An enquiry may also require children to employ empathy and imagination, both of which have to be informed by the knowledge of the context and content of the enquiry. However, there does need to be a balance between the teaching of science skills, through scientific enquiry, and the teaching and learning of scientific content. This balance is essential to the science curriculum, because − as I have already stated − not all science can be learned through enquiry. Therefore, although scientific enquiry is essential to the science curriculum, and is particularly motivating for the reluctant learner, owing to its hands-on, 'no right or wrong answer' approach, the study of biology, chemistry and physics is of equal importance. The skill of the teacher is in making the study of these strands of the curriculum as interesting, motivating and inspiring as that of scientific enquiry.

Science 2, 3 and 4: the important bits

There is an adage that says:

If it moves, it's biology,
If it smells, it's chemistry,
And if it doesn't work, it's physics.

I certainly hope that isn't true of modern-day science (if it were ever true!), but it does explain the foci of the content aspect of the National Curriculum Order for Science. Science 2, 'Life processes and living things', contains requirements relating to biology; Science 3, 'Materials and their properties', relates to chemistry; and Science 4, 'Physical processes', relates to physics. Within each strand, concepts to study are proposed for each key stage, and links are made between key stages. For example, in Science 2 at Key Stage 1, pupils are taught that animals, including humans, move, feed, grow, use their senses and reproduce; in Key Stage 2 the pupils expand on this by learning the names of the life processes and studying them in more detail.

It is beyond the scope of this book to go into detail about each requirement at each key stage, but it is important that teachers develop an understanding of the requirements as a whole and, in turn, seek out interesting and motivating ways to deliver the requirements to their pupils. Scientific content must not be treated solely as science facts to be instructed, learned and recalled at a later date; the National Curriculum Order (Qualifications and Curriculum Authority, 1999a) states this explicitly by detailing the types of activity that pupils in each key stage should be involved in. These include activities that refer directly to scientific enquiry and ones that relate to the acquisition of science facts. The requirements for the activities for the teaching and learning of scientific content can be summarized thus:

Pupils at **Key Stage 1** should be engaged in activities that involve:

- observation, exploration and questioning;
- working together;
- linking simple scientific ideas;
- using reference materials;
- sharing ideas;
- communicating ideas through language, drawings, charts and tables;
- an awareness of health and safety issues.

At **Key Stage 2** the activities expand on those at Key Stage 1 by now requiring pupils:

- to make links between ideas;
- to apply their developing knowledge and understanding of scientific ideas to familiar phenomena, everyday things and personal health;
- to think about the positive and negative effects of scientific developments;
- to use a broader range of reference sources;
- to talk about their work in science;
- to communicate their ideas using a wider range of scientific language, conventional diagrams, charts and graphs.

At **Key Stage 3** the requirements are developed further by requiring the pupils:

- to build on their scientific knowledge and understanding;
- to make connections between different areas of science;
- to use scientific ideas and models to explain phenomena and events;
- to use scientific ideas and models to understand a range of familiar applications of science;
- to consider the positive and negative effects of scientific and technological developments on the environment and in other contexts;
- to consider the views of others;
- to consider why opinions may differ;
- to select and use a wider range of reference sources;
- to learn how scientists work together on present-day scientific developments;
- to know the importance of experimental evidence in supporting scientific ideas.

Finally, at **Key Stage 4** the content aspect of the National Curriculum Order for Science is delivered through activities that require pupils:

- a study a wider range of scientific ideas;
- to consider scientific ideas in greater depth;
- to explore how technological advances relate to the scientific ideas behind them;
- to consider the power and limitations of science;
- to relate science to industrial, ethical and environmental issues;
- to consider how and why different groups have differing views about the role of science;
- to use and select appropriate reference sources;
- to communicate their ideas clearly and precisely in a variety of ways;
- to consider how scientists work together to develop new ideas;
- to consider how new theories may, at first, provoke controversy;
- to consider the extent to which social and cultural contexts may affect the acceptance of new theories.

The requirements summarized above provide excellent guidance for the teacher in devising a relevant, interesting and exciting curriculum for all learners. The documentation sets out clearly the types of activity that can enable pupils to learn *the important bits* of science. Through this guidance, the importance of how scientific facts were arrived at through the work of scientists, and the role of reflection and discussion in the development of scientific knowledge, can be clearly appreciated. The requirements emphasize the value of communication, talking with others and thinking about science, to the study of science and illustrate the significance of the connections between the study of science content and that of science enquiry.

6 Some basic techniques

It is imperative that we are able to inspire pupils to engage in the science curriculum, particularly if we are to interest the reluctant learner. The ideas presented so far in the book may all interest different pupils in different ways; unfortunately, there is no one, sure-fire winner for all pupils! What interests one pupil may put another pupil off altogether, and so we must constantly search for ideas that inspire us and try them out with the pupils. In this chapter I present some basic techniques for encouraging independence in the pupils, from making suggestions for their own scientific enquiries and explorations to aiding their research, from articulating their ideas to using role play to explore their ideas. This independence is important to learning, especially for reluctant learners who may see no need to engage in learning, and yet to merely ask a pupil what he or she would like to study or is interested in may result in a shrug of the shoulders or to suggestions that do not lead to meaningful learning in science. The basic techniques I am presenting here encourage independence and involvement in directing the curriculum, yet are founded on the basic needs of an appropriate course of science study. I have found each technique to be simple, successful and easy to put into practice with pupils of all ages.

Asking questions

One of the requirements of the National Curriculum Order for Science (Qualifications and Curriculum Authority 1999a) is for pupils to ask questions that can be investigated scientifically, and yet devising such questions is quite a complex skill to develop. I have used the technique I am describing here to generate a range of questions that can be answered through research, through present knowledge and through investigation, with different age groups, including teachers on a training day. I remember reading about a similar technique that inspired me many years ago but have long since forgotten its origin. It inspired me because of its simplicity and the way in which it generates questions that can be quite exciting, and also because it can begin a debate about the science behind simple artefacts we use in everyday life without questioning either their origin or how they work.

I always use the activity with small groups or pairs, to capitalize on the different ideas the members of the group are most likely to hold. To begin the activity, I provide each group with an object – for example, a pair of glasses, a packet of washing powder tablets, a sachet of sauce. I then give the group (or pair) a set amount of time in which to write down their questions about the object; I do give a number of questions for the pupils to aim for, but this is dependent on the age of the pupils. The one rule for the activity is that everyone's questions are added; there are no correct or incorrect questions.

The pupils are then instructed to sort the questions under three headings:

1. questions we already know the answer to;
2. questions we can find the answer to through research;
3. questions we can find the answer to through investigation.

The groups are then asked to ensure that there is at least one question under each heading. Depending on the age of the pupils, I may discuss the lists with the whole class or may support individual groups. The pupils then use their lists to choose questions to be researched through secondary sources, and questions on which to base an investigation.

This technique provides a focus for the pupils to generate their own questions but is not prescriptive – that is, it is not the teacher who is outlining an investigation, but the pupils. It ensures that the entire group is engaged in the task of asking questions about the object and all ideas are of equal value. It is a technique that puts the pupils in charge of their learning, as they are asking the questions that interest them, and they decide on the areas to research or to investigate, yet it ensures that what is suggested meets the learning objective set by the teacher. The pupils will therefore set the context for their investigations and will use the necessary scientific skills for a purpose that they have identified, to solve a problem they have generated. The fact that the pupils themselves set the agenda is particularly important for engaging and motivating the reluctant learner.

Question, answer and note boards

Another technique I have used for generating questions for research is simply the use of a question board, as suggested by Feasey (1999). I use a laminated card with a wipe-on, wipe-off pen for pupils to record the questions that interest them. I limit the space available for writing in, as demonstrated in Figure 6.1, to encourage the generation of simply worded, concise questions. The board also provides suggestions for question openers to encourage the pupils in their thoughts and to aid their formulation of questions. The layout of the board ensures that the reluctant learner, who may also be a reluctant writer, appreciates that the activity is not dependent on copious amounts of writing.

Following the generation of questions to be answered through research, either by using the techniques described here for asking questions or by other means, it is crucial to ensure the pupils are able to answer their questions accurately and succinctly, in order to maintain interest and motivation. When faced with a wealth of information regarding a certain concept or topic, reluctant learners will often make one of two choices: either not to engage in the activity at all, or merely to copy out the whole text, thus not interacting with the text or answering the original question they were interested in. In order to aid the pupils in their research and to avoid the copying out of vasts amount of text, I use two boards similar to the question board: an answer board that accompanies the question board (Figure 6.2) and a note board for recording key ideas or facts in a text (Figure 6.3). Again I have found these boards, as proposed by Feasey (1999), to be the most effective techniques for enabling pupils of all ages to record meaningful research using texts.

The boards are presented in the same way as the question board, having limited space for recording, thus requiring the pupil to identify the main points of interest in the text.

Write down 10 questions about ....

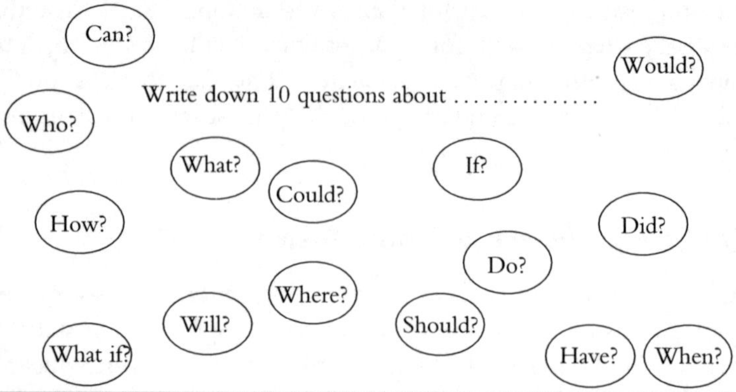

1	
2	
3	
4	
5	
6	
7	
8	
9	
10	
Notes	

Figure 6.1 Question board (adapted from Feasey 1999, p. 89)

Use this board to answer the 10 questions on your question board	
1	
2	
3	
4	
5	
6	
7	
8	
9	
10	
Notes	

Figure 6.2 Answer board (adapted from Feasey 1999, p. 91.)

When you have read the information, make a list of the 10 key ideas or key facts.	
1	
2	
3	
4	
5	
6	
7	
8	
9	
10	

Figure 6.3 Note board (adapted from Feasey 1999, p. 97.)

The information the pupils record may be handled in various ways. The teacher may share the list and ask relevant questions about it, the pupils may present the information to another group or to the whole class, or it may be used as a plan for a formal, factual piece of writing.

Mind-mapping, brainstorming and thought showers

I use mind-mapping and brainstorming as two distinct techniques, though other people use them to indicate the same activity. I am also informed that brainstorming is a politically incorrect and out-of-date term that has been replaced by the term *thought shower*. However, as yet, 'thought shower' is not a term I am comfortable with! I use mind-mapping as a technique for demonstrating present knowledge about a concept or area and brainstorming for committing half-ideas and questions to paper. Both are excellent techniques for provoking discussion within groups and within a whole class, and thus for inspiring further investigation and exploration.

Both techniques begin with the placing of a key word or visual image in the centre of a large piece of paper. For mind-mapping, further known key words, images, phrases or sentences are placed around the centre word (see Figure 6.4). Links are then made between the words, phrases, etc. using lines or arrows on which the connecting ideas are written. Colour may be used to code themes and associations, and to make different ideas stand out from the text. For brainstorming, the ideas and questions are usually linked to the centre key word or image only (Figure 6.5). For me, mind-mapping demonstrates current thinking, whereas brainstorming is an effective way of clarifying ideas, generating new ideas and questions, and suggesting problems to solve.

Mind-mapping and brainstorming encourage pupils to be creative in their thinking and remove the need for formal recording involving the writing of copious notes. I find that the pupils become more willing to share their ideas, as the techniques appear to be informal and non-threatening. Even the most reluctant of pupils begin to contribute and exercise their mind during these activities!

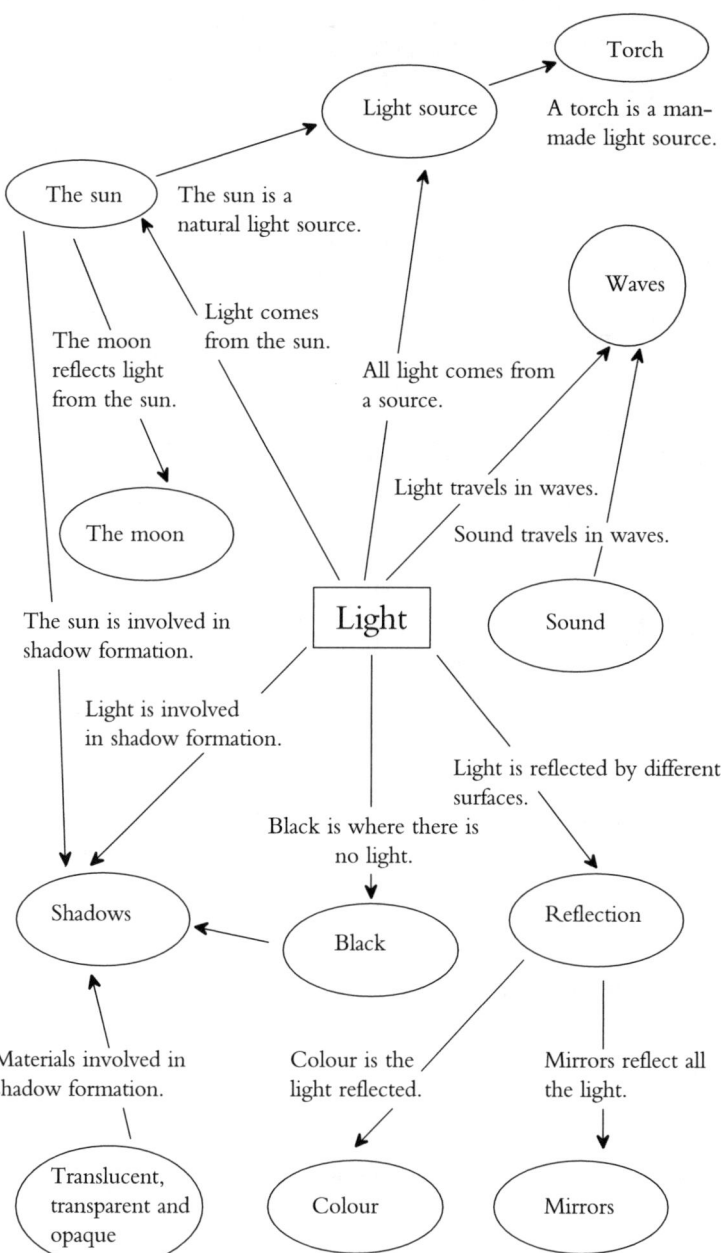

Figure 6.4 An example of mind-mapping

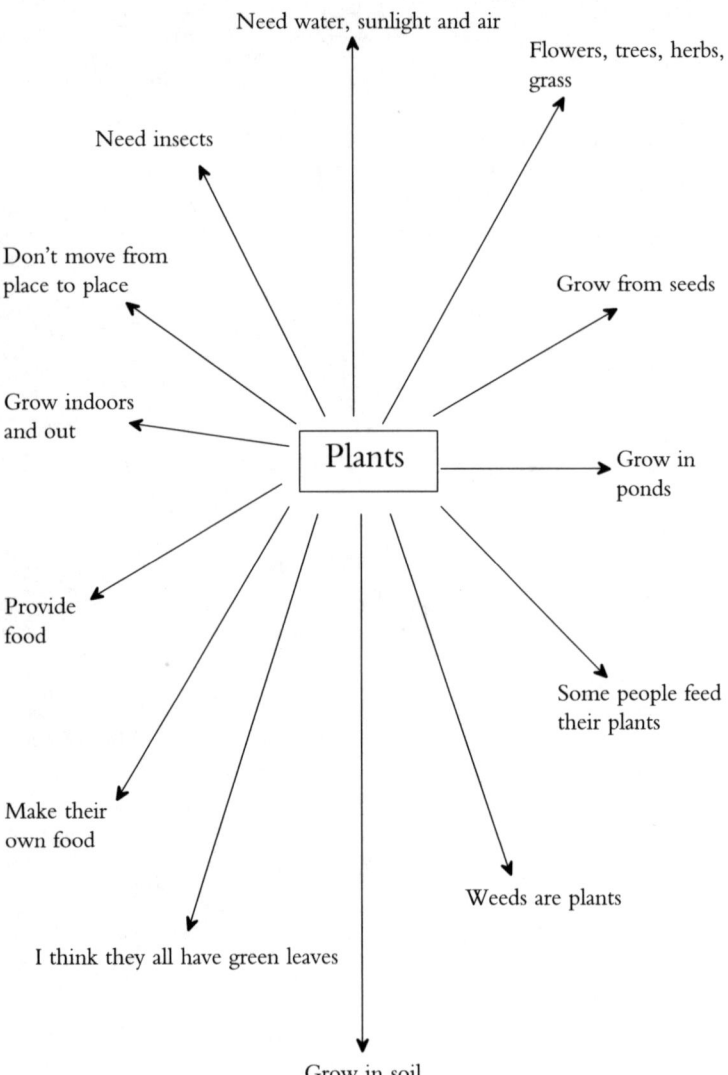

Figure 6.5 An example of brainstorming (thought shower)

Drama and role-play

Drama and role-play activities are excellent ways of engaging the reluctant learner. They are versatile techniques that can be used most effectively in science. They can be used:

- to encourage pupils to demonstrate their current knowledge and understanding of scientific facts;
- to enable pupils to communicate their own scientific interpretations;
- to develop scientific knowledge and attitudes;
- to generate ideas for scientific exploration and investigation;
- to generate suggestions for visits to environments outside the classroom.

Drama or role-play activities may therefore be based on scientific evidence provided by the teacher, scientific understanding provided by the pupils, or evidence provided by the pupil through research or investigation. Used in this way, the activities provide an exciting and stimulating medium through which to draw together learning from various sources.

There are various different drama and role-play activities that can be used in science. These include:

- *Hot-seating.* One pupil takes on the role of a scientist or a character interested in a particular scientific discovery and other pupils ask questions about his or her life and work. The pupil taking on the role will need to have researched the character and to be able to answer the questions truthfully. For younger pupils it may be more appropriate for the teacher or another adult to take on the role.
- *Role-playing* of a scientific discovery. Again, prior knowledge of the discovery and the events leading up to it will be needed by the pupils involved.
- *Modelled role-play.* The pupils act out a recognized model in science – for example, the parts of an electric circuit or the molecules in water in the three states. This activity requires the pupils either to have prior knowledge of the model and to interpret it in their own way or to be given detailed instruction by the teacher during the role-play.
- *Discussion cards.* The teacher prepares a set of cards giving

information about a specific scientific theme. Each pupil is given a card that contains some information about the theme being studied. Using the different pieces of information, the pupils are able to take part in a discussion about the theme – for example, whether cloning of humans should be allowed.

- *Role cards.* Again the teacher prepares a set of cards on which different roles are detailed. Each pupil is given a card, and pupils assume the role detailed, whether the role necessitates being for or against the scientific theme they will discuss. Using the information on his or her card, each pupil takes part in the ensuing discussion about an issue related to science, such as the building of a nuclear power plant nearby. The roles will include those of a resident, a scientist, a builder, etc.

- *What happened next?* The teacher provides a problem or tells part of a story about a discovery, and the children act out what they consider to be the likely outcome of the problem or ending to the story. This activity will enable the pupils to draw on previous knowledge and to apply it to this new situation.

It can be appreciated how drama and role-play are powerful techniques for engaging learners and promoting discussion and exploration in science. The techniques may begin with unstructured play for the youngest pupils, then move on to structured play, and can certainly continue to Key Stage 4 and beyond. The activities can be extended to provide the pupils with the opportunity to handle and manipulate objects within the drama activities, to act out their own ideas and theories, and to apply their developing knowledge to a whole range of real contexts. For reluctant learners particularly they provide another context for increasing their understanding and promote their confidence in expressing their discoveries, thoughts and ideas.

Solving problems

Providing pupils with a real-life problem to solve is a particularly motivating way to provoke discussion and exploration in science. This has already been demonstrated through the ice-lolly activity suggested in Chapter 4. There are many, many other problems that could be presented, from 'where is the best place in the classroom for keeping a plant, given by a special person, that thrives in a warm temperature but does not grow under direct sunlight?', to persuading the Head to allow chewing gum in school. Such activities inspire pupils to use their scientific knowledge to provide evidence for a solution to the problem and to communicate their solution to a real-life audience.

In order to suggest the best place for the plant to thrive, the pupils may suggest taking the temperature of different areas of the classroom throughout the day to find the warmest place, while checking that the sites are not in the path of direct sunlight. Or they may suggest the use of a data-logging device to record the temperatures over twenty-four hours. In other words, the problem set will generate discussion and theory building, and lead on to the planning of an investigation with a real purpose and a real outcome, rather than the teacher merely instructing the pupils in the skill of using a thermometer or data-logging device.

The problem of persuading the Head to allow chewing gum in school may suggest research into the benefits and drawbacks of chewing gum, contact with chewing-gum manufacturers and investigations into the cleaning of teeth. It will require the pupils to communicate the findings to the Head and will lead on to literacy work with the writing of a persuasive argument! Again, this is a case of a real-life problem being used to generate meaningful science and science exploration.

The skills needed to engage in problem solving in science can be summarized as:

- identifying the problem – this may be teacher generated or pupil generated;
- understanding the problem – what the question is that the problem is asking;
- suggesting possible solutions to the problem;
- planning ways to gather evidence for the solution to the problem;
- gathering the evidence – through investigation, exploration and/or research;

- reviewing the evidence – what the evidence is telling us about the proposed solution;
- presenting the solution to the problem, together with the evidence for the solution proposed.

Further ideas for problems to solve are given in the next part of the book, which looks at the place of science within the curriculum as a whole.

Part Three

Science and the Whole Curriculum

7 Using science as a context for learning

Science is an excellent vehicle for providing the basis for a topic connecting learning in different areas of the curriculum, the approach known at the cross-curricular topic. It is able to offer numerous opportunities for related work in many areas across the curriculum, although this is more relevant to pupils in the Foundation Stage and Key Stages 1 and 2 of the National Curriculum than pupils in Key Stages 3 and 4. Science is also a suitable vehicle for the development of the key skills that are used across the curriculum, and indeed into adult life, and is a meaningful context for the study of other individual subjects such as literacy and numeracy. It is therefore a versatile subject that can be studied on its own, can be used to facilitate learning in other subjects and can be employed both to use and to develop a range of key skills. This part of the book is therefore concerned with this versatility, especially where it is used to motivate the reluctant learner into engaging with the curriculum in general and with science in particular.

Throughout the book so far, I have stressed the existence of the relevant documentation for science, which sets out the needs of the science curriculum, and that these needs are the minimum requirement for our pupils to study. I have also emphasized that it is the role of teachers to interpret the documentation and to use the contents as a base for their science teaching; it cannot be overstated how vital this interpretation of the requirements is for encouraging reluctant learners and to ensure that a relevant, meaningful and accessible programme is made available to them. Irrelevant or badly planned activities and contexts will not engage learners and so learning opportunities will not be taken up; this is true of any subjects in which learners are reluctant to engage in the planned activities. The use of science as meaningful context for learning will promote the integration of the curriculum offered and will lead to a much-needed coherence in teaching and learning for reluctant learners.

Cross-curricular planning

Cross-curricular planning is an approach to planning whereby several subjects are taught through a common topic, such as 'The Theatre', or 'The Garden Centre'. This used to be a very popular approach to planning in the primary school but in recent years has declined in popularity. However, with the introduction of *Excellence and Enjoyment* (Department for Education and Skills 2003) it is becoming much more acceptable once again. It is an approach that brings creativity to the whole curriculum and increases its coherence by capitalizing on common or complementary knowledge, skills and understanding contained in different subject areas, and provides the much-needed relevance of the work being delivered. I must caution here that the advantages and disadvantages of this approach to the curriculum have been debated for many years; there are those who favour the approach for the reasons set out above, and those who criticize it for being undemanding, and failing to provide progression in the learning, and because, they say, subjects lose their identity and characteristics. However, the approach can be most successful if the teacher is mindful of these considerations that led to its falling out of favour. Cross-curricular planning is an effective vehicle for learning if it:

- is well thought out;
- is well planned;
- is structured;
- is based on common themes, skills and understandings;
- links together appropriate subject areas;
- retains and emphasizes the individuality of each subject area.

The approach is indicated strongly within the Foundation Stage requirements, where the science curriculum is detailed alongside design and technology, geography, history and ICT.

The approach is used to provide the pupils with relevance for their learning by making the links between the subject areas explicit; this approach is a vital one for reluctant learners of any age. It enables the pupils to focus on the *process* of their learning rather than on the mere acquisition of facts in different subject areas, and provides a meaning for their studies. I will therefore make suggestions in this part of the book for how science may be linked to literacy, to numeracy, to ICT and to the foundation subjects of the National Curriculum, and through this begin to look at cross-curricular planning, ending with an overview of two of my favourite cross-curricular topics: 'A Victorian Washday' and 'Science and Fast Food'.

Key skills

There are many key skills that are needed in all subject areas and into adult life; within the 1999 National Curriculum handbook for primary teachers (Qualifications and Curriculum Authority 1999a) they are listed as:

- communication;
- the application of number;
- information technology;
- working with others;
- improving own learning and performance;
- problem solving.

In addition to these, emphasis is also given within the document to the promotion of thinking skills. Five aspects to be focused upon are identified:

- information processing skills;
- reasoning skills;
- enquiry skills;
- creative thinking skills;
- evaluation skills.

Even more skills are to be considered! These are:

- choice;
- decision making;

- critical thinking;
- respect.

Quite a long list, and yet the links between these skills, the skills of scientific enquiry and the attitudes indicated in science can clearly be seen. Science study is therefore an ideal context for these skills to be both developed and used, and so, yet again, the need for a relevant, interesting and exciting science curriculum is indicated, in order for all learners, including reluctant learners, to be able to master them. As a result, although science is a valuable, worthwhile and interesting subject to study in its own right – for all the reasons already stated in the book – its value also lies in the many opportunities it provides for developing the range of key skills – indeed, skills that are developed and used without the learners even realizing that they are using such skills!

Using the key skills

I have used the activity I am about to describe with teachers at a training day looking at the development of key skills in different curriculum subjects. My focus was on using science to identify the key skills in practice. After having carried out the activity, the teachers were invited to identify the key skills they had needed to use; I think all of us were amazed at the full range of skills employed! The activity is a lovely open task that all age groups could engage in and is a good example of the type of activity essential for engaging the reluctant learner. It provides a meaning for carrying out the activity by posing a problem to be solved that is set in a real-life context.

The problem
The activity, like almost all my activities, was carried out in small groups. Each group was provided with a copy of a letter presented in a sealed envelope. Incidentally, if you use this activity with a class of pupils, it would be worth posting the letters to school, to add authenticity to the problem. The wording of the text would also need to be made age-appropriate, as I am presenting the adult version I used with the teachers on the training day. The letter read:

Room 7
Flat 9
Rockingham House
The Lanes Campus
Newtown University
Newtown, N23 7EC

Hi Mum and Dad,

University is great! The course is going OK and the flat's brill. I've loads of new friends so don't worry, Mum.

Actually I have got a bit of a problem. I'm ever so confused. You know I've never done any washing (thanks, Mum), so I don't know what to use! I've narrowed it down to three choices, 'cos the local shop sells branded tablets – they're £3.26 for 32 washes; another branded name, but this is a powder with added conditioner at £2.20 for 1 kg (does 24 washes apparently); and their own-brand tablets at £2.90 for 30 washes. Which is best? I want my clothes clean but don't want to spend too much. What do I do?

Got to go, going to the pub, ring you soon.

Love, John

The solution

The groups were then asked to consider how they could help John with his problem. Each group decided that an investigation was needed and set about coming up with a fair test to compare the powder and the two types of tablet.

The language used by the groups throughout the activity was excellent, with all teachers fully engaged in the task and in writing a letter back to John to explain his best option and the reasons for this. Each group developed a slightly different investigation, although almost all the results indicated that one option was the best. (Sorry, I can't remember which one; you'll have to find out yourself by carrying out your own fair test!)

Following the testing, and the reporting back to the whole group of how they solved the problem and what the results of the test were, the whole group evaluated the task and listed the skills used as follows:

- *Problem solving.* The task itself was a given problem to solve. The participants of the course also had to solve problems within their work: how to compare a tablet with powder, how to replicate the motion of a washing machine, etc.
- *Communication skills.* Communication skills had to be used throughout the task, from reading the letter setting out the problem, discussing the problem, talking to each other about the work and then to writing back to John.
- *Information processing skills.* Again these were used throughout, from processing the information given in the letter, information given on the packaging of the washing products to processing the information they provided through their investigation.
- *Working with others.* The task was presented as a group task that required a group response, and so the participants naturally worked with each other within the group.
- *Creative thinking.* As the groups began to consider a solution to the problem, they certainly used their creative thinking skills to work round the problem set.
- *Reasoning skills.* Reasoning skills were also used throughout the task, to think around the problem, possible solutions and in presenting participants' own ideas to the group.
- *Enquiry skills.* The activity required the use of enquiry skills throughout.
- *Choice* and *decision making.* The participants exercised choice and decision making in deciding the exact investigation plan to follow, in detailing the equipment to use and in determining how much powder to use, how long to immerse the fabric, how many times to agitate the powder solution, etc.
- *The application of number.* The activity presented many opportunities to apply the use of number, including the comparison of the prices of the washing powder products in relation to the number of expected washes, timing during the investigation, use of standard or non-standard measures for weight, etc.
- *Evaluation skills.* Following the investigation, the groups evaluated their work, and the work of others, to consider both their approach to the task and their findings.

- *Improving learning and performance.* The evaluations led to each group considering how they had approached the problem, how they had addressed the issues and how they could have improved their own performance.
- *Critical thinking.* Critical thinking was needed throughout the task in order to address the problem and identify ways to find a solution.
- *Respect.* Respect was shown throughout the task: respect for each other and each other's ideas, respect for the task, respect for the equipment and for the room itself.
- *Information technology.* Information technology was used to prepare the letter of reply and was available for participants to obtain further information about the washing products and how a washing machine works.

It can be appreciated that this quite simple task required knowledge of scientific enquiry and the skills needed to plan and carry out an investigation, yet also required the use of a range of skills that cross all boundaries of the curriculum. The teaching of each skill in isolation would appear to be difficult and pointless when the whole range can be developed through such activities as this one. However, one or more of the skills may prove difficult for the reluctant learner, and in turn this makes a group solution to the problem more difficult to achieve. It is therefore important for the teacher to identify activities, such as this one, that involve using a wide range of key skills, and to identify other, less demanding tasks that provide opportunities for the use of a more limited range of skills.

8 Science and the core subjects

The core subjects of the National Curriculum are English, maths and science, and, as core subjects, need to have a greater amount of curriculum time spent on them than on the rest of the curriculum. When the National Literacy and Numeracy Strategies were introduced into the primary curriculum, teachers began to identify ways in which other subjects, including science, could be linked with English and maths and the subjects used to complement each other. In reality, what was identified was the symbiotic nature of science and literacy and science and numeracy: science could provide a meaningful context for the practical application of the skills of literacy and numeracy, whereas literacy and numeracy could provide the skills needed for pupils to fully access science study. In practice this means that skills specific to English and maths are taught during literacy and numeracy sessions and then used – that is, applied – in other subjects, including science. Science may also be used as the vehicle within the literacy and numeracy lesson for making the skills learning *real*. As I have stated many times, it is this understanding of the need for the skills and their application to be put into real-life situations that motivates and engages reluctant learners.

When planning the learning, the teacher needs to remember that the aim of the science lesson is to develop the pupils' scientific knowledge, understanding, skills and/or attitudes, while offering opportunities for applying learning from literacy and numeracy in a scientific context, whereas the aim of the literacy lesson is the development of literacy. The links between the subjects ensure that the subject areas are *complementary* to one another; they add unity to the curriculum for the learner, but the subjects still retain their own identity. Linking the subjects in this way therefore promotes meaningful learning in each subject, together with the development of the key skills relating to communication and the application of number.

Science and literacy

The interplay between science and literacy as described can be a very powerful way to motivate the reluctant learner. The development of literacy skills will empower pupils to engage with science more readily, whereas the use of science as a context for literacy may encourage fuller participation in literacy activities. The use of literacy with regard to text, to develop an interest and enthusiasm in science, will be demonstrated shortly; literacy skills are also needed to enable the learner to succeed across the science curriculum by enabling him or her to access sources of information and to communicate ideas in written and oral forms. Conversely, using science as a context within literacy development provides the learner with a real-life context for learning, thus giving the learner a reason for the study or skill acquisition.

It is imperative that each subject retains its own identity. One way to make sure that they do is to ensure that both the teacher and the learners are able to distinguish the focus of the lesson and the learning to take place within the lesson. The learning objective for each lesson must therefore be worded clearly to set out whether the learning is related to a science development or a literacy development; I now provide two examples to clarify this distinction.

Example 1: literacy development
Lesson objective: To write a set of simple instructions.
Science context: Pupils to write instructions for someone else to follow in order to be able to recreate an investigation they have planned and carried out in class.

Example 2: science development
Lesson objective: To identify to what extent the conclusions of an investigation support a prediction made.
Literacy skill: Presenting a persuasive argument, verbal or written, using the appropriate vocabulary of persuasion.

The two examples make it obvious how science and literacy are complementary in practice and how the connection between them is a meaningful one. The examples also demonstrate how the learning in both subjects can benefit from the relationship. In example 1, science provides a meaningful context for the development of the skill of instruction writing, whereas example 2 demonstrates a real-life need for the acquisition of the language of persuasion, as without it learners may not be able to fully demonstrate their thinking about how their conclusions support the prediction they had offered. For reluctant learners meaning is given to the curriculum they are engaged in, and they can more readily understand why they are being taught the skills of literacy.

There are many, many examples of where science can support literacy and where literacy skills are demonstrated through scientific activity. The following is my top ten list.

1. recording conclusions to an investigation in the style of a newspaper report;
2. rewriting the story of a scientist as an autobiography (i.e. the pupil as the scientist);
3. using bullet points when presenting information from a text;
4. informing others of the conclusions from an investigation via a formal or informal letter;
5. recording science knowledge in the form of a poem;
6. generating a list of questions to ask a scientist;
7. preparing a glossary of scientific terms related to a specific concept;
8. labelling a scientific diagram;
9. preparing an information poster;
10. writing a science quiz.

These top ten suggestions all provide interesting and exciting ways to record science, ways that are motivational for the reluctant learner, and do not rely on merely writing a science report using a given format. The suggestions all use a recognized genre of writing, thus providing a reason for the learner to know the features of the genre chosen.

Oracy

The top ten ideas for where science can support the acquisition and use of literacy skills do not include an oral retelling of a scientific activity, but oracy, the skills of speaking and listening, is an extremely important area of English (and therefore literacy) and is an essential skill in science, as was described in Part 2 of the book. The skill is essential for science and scientific studies as it enables pupils both to express their ideas and their understandings in science and to carry out discussions with their peers and adults; this again reflects the complementary nature of science and literacy. There are many activities within science that can be used to develop the skills of oracy – for example:

- discussions – about a scientific issue or discovery;
- drama and role-play activities – as described in Part 2 of the book;
- presentations – of ideas, research, etc.;
- quizzes – questions using scientific vocabulary and/or concepts that require oral answers to be shared with the class;
- questions – lists of questions generated and asked of an expert, a scientist or an adult in role as a famous scientist;
- paired conversations – about ideas, discoveries, investigations, etc.

The need for pupils to increasingly develop their oracy skills cannot be overstated, not only within literacy and science but also across the whole curriculum. For the reluctant learner the development of oracy may be what is needed for the pupil to be able to demonstrate his or her knowledge and understanding of, and attitudes towards, science. Well-developed speaking and listening skills are also needed to promote empathy and respect for others. It is therefore essential that the teacher identifies many suitable activities involving speaking and listening. As I have made clear in Part Two of the book, I believe that science is a social activity that is vastly improved by pupils working together, sharing ideas, discussing solutions, comparing results and agreeing the interpretation of results, and so almost all the activities in the book will impact on pupils' oracy if delivered in the ways suggested.

Using texts

One of my favourite vehicles for motivating reluctant learners is text. There are many texts that can be used to inspire and suggest further activities in science:

- fictional stories, e.g. *Cinderella* (see Chapter 1);
- true stories, e.g. the story of Ben Franklin and his work (see below);
- letters as described in Chapter 7;
- posters, e.g. fire safety posters;
- adverts, e.g. adverts for sporting activities during the school holidays;
- poetry, e.g. 'Dirty T-shirt' by Michael Rosen (2000).

The use of text is twofold: within science, an appropriate text can provide a meaningful context for scientific enquiry or a humorous introduction to a concept to be investigated; within literacy, the use of a text for inspiring scientific work can reinforce the need for reading skills to be acquired. Both these overt uses for texts are most important for motivating reluctant learners. There are many, many texts that can be used, and some will obviously be more useful and motivational than others. Thus, as with most of the ideas presented in the book, the key to using texts is the skill of the teacher in identifying a suitable text and the work it may inspire.

The use of fictional stories has been considered earlier in the book (*Cinderella* and *Winnie the Pooh*, in Part 1 of the book), and the use of true stories can be illustrated here by the life and work of Ben Franklin.

Ben Franklin

Benjamin Franklin was an American born in 1706 in Boston, one of seventeen children; he died in 1790 at the age of 84. As Franklin grew up, he became involved in printing, publishing and writing through becoming an apprentice printer at the age of 12. He taught himself to read and write, and later moved to Philadelphia to find work as a printer in his own right, before moving to England to raise money to set up his own company. He later returned to Philadelphia and soon went into business with a friend; his work made him quite a rich man.

Franklin was also a scientist. In 1746 he became interested in electricity and electrical theories. One of his friends in England had sent an electrical machine to the Library Company of Philadelphia; Franklin and three of his American friends then began to carry out investigations into electrical phenomena and together they developed many of the terms we use today in discussing electricity: positive, negative, battery, conductor, etc. It was for his reports of the electrical experiments he carried out, and the theories he proposed, that he is best known as a scientist.

Franklin was also an inventor, known for inventing a heater to replace open fires and for inventing bifocal spectacles. During the course of his life, Franklin ran a fire company, a library, an insurance company, an academy and a hospital, and yet he was not well liked at the time. (Adapted from Ben Franklin, www. crystalinks.com, 2004.)

The story of Ben Franklin is obviously much longer than the summary I have given here. It can be offered to pupils in a long or short format and can be used in many ways in different areas of the curriculum. In science it may be used purely as a story of how a scientist lived and worked, it may be used to direct the pupils to carry out related research or investigations, or it may be used to inspire them to suggest their own follow-up work to the reading of the story. Pupils may be inspired to:

- research more about Ben Franklin, including his life and work;
- research electrical theories;
- role-play Ben Franklin and imagine why he was so active in his life;
- carry out their own investigations using electrical components;
- research the difference between printing in the eighteenth century and printing today;
- compare different spectacles, including bifocals.

Other non-fiction texts, such as letters, posters and adverts may motivate pupils to respond in many ways, for example they may:

- plan and carry out a related investigation e.g. the cleaning effect on teeth of chewing gum;
- research a topic, e.g. the effects of exercise on the body;
- provide the answer to a question posed in a letter, e.g. the ingredients needed to prepare a healthy sandwich;
- present information for use by a younger child, e.g. using a fire safety poster for adults to make a poster for display in Key Stage 1.

I particularly enjoy presenting poetry to a class and then following this up with related science work. Poetry is a successful stimulus as it is often a short piece of writing that engages a child because of its simplicity and often its humour. Used skilfully the content can be discussed and many questions posed. This then leads onto meaningful investigations and research, together with the inspiration to carry out other learning activities in a variety of subjects.

Once you begin to work in this way you will be able to look at a variety of texts in a new way and you (and your pupils) will increasingly be able to select appropriate texts and build up a much broader list of follow-up work than the examples I have presented here.

It can be appreciated from this brief consideration of texts how motivational their usage can be and how many different scientific activities can be suggested by them. For reluctant learners the scientific activities are given a purpose and thus a reason for their completion by the learner. Allowing the pupils to suggest their own follow-up to the texts ensures that the pupils take ownership of the scientific activity and are responsible for its completion. The activities suggested also promote the development and use of one or more of the key skills outlined in Chapter 7, as they may require the pupils:

- to identify a problem to solve;
- to use their communication skills;
- to process information;
- work with others;
- to think creatively;
- to reason – thinking around the problem, the solution and sharing their ideas with others;

- to use their enquiry skills;
- to make choices and decisions;
- to use application of number;
- to use their skills of evaluation;
- to consider how to improve their learning and performance;
- to think critically about the text, the problem and the research they find;
- to show respect for others;
- to use information technology.

Science and numeracy

Many of the reasons cited for the use of science within literacy and the need for literacy skills within science also apply to the consideration of the interplay between science and numeracy.

- The development of numeracy skills will empower pupils within scientific enquiry.
- Numeracy skills are needed within science – for example, the ability to present information accurately on a line graph.
- The use of science as a context for numeracy may motivate reluctant learners in their maths work.
- Using science as a context within numeracy development again provides learners with a real–life need for acquiring the skills.

The need to distinguish between the focus of a lesson and the learning taking place within the lesson is again important for both the teacher and the learner, and so the wording of the objective is important for indicating whether the proposed learning is related to a science development or a numeracy development; the two examples below clarify this distinction with respect to numeracy and science:

Example 1: numeracy development

Lesson objective: To suggest suitable units with which to estimate or measure time.

Science context: Pupils carry out their own investigations into paper shapes falling (gyrocopters) and decide how to time the drop – stopwatch using seconds, non-standard measures, etc.

Example 2: science development

Lesson objective: To communicate results using an appropriate method of communication.

Numeracy skill: The accurate presentation of a block graph or pictogram.

As with science and literacy, these examples clearly demonstrate the complementary nature of science and numeracy, and that the relationship is also a naturally occurring, valid one in which both subjects benefit, and through which pupils benefit through meaning given to the curriculum and the teaching of skills relevant to a successful outcome to their work. Again I include a list of ten activities that use both the context of science and a mathematical skill.

1. accurately measuring plant growth over a period of time;
2. using a thermometer accurately to record temperatures in the classroom, around school and into the school garden;
3. presenting results using a line graph;
4. for younger pupils, using positional language ('above', 'below', 'behind') to describe the inhabitants of the school garden environment;
5. use of estimation followed by accurate reading of a force meter when investigating forces in the classroom;
6. using a tally chart to record data, then transferring the data on to a graph to display the data and to identify a pattern in the data;
7. using mean, mode, median to answer questions about pattern in the results;
8. accurately measuring the angle of change each hour when observing the shadow of a stick in the playground throughout the day;
9. using a Venn diagram to record the properties of given materials;
10. using fractions or percentages when reaching conclusions from results.

For me, the mathematical ten above are all practical applications of a mathematical skill that need to be understood by learners in order to be used appropriately. The acquisition of each skill is warranted for the learner to proceed in his or her scientific understanding, and so the skills are not learned and used in isolation but are needed for a purpose, and it is this again that gives meaning to reluctant learners for the work being presented to them and motivates them to engage in the learning.

9 Science and the foundation subjects

The examples of activities given in Part Three of this book demonstrate the connections between science and literacy, and science and numeracy. Science may also be linked to other individual subject areas in the curriculum – for example, with history when comparing the properties of traditional fabrics with the properties of modern artificial fabrics, or with PE when investigating the effects of exercise on the heart rate and breathing rate. Almost all curriculum areas can be linked with science in this way for all the reasons cited in earlier chapters – adding coherence to the learning, providing a real context for the learning and giving a reason for the learning to take place. Although this linking of subject areas is much more difficult to achieve in the secondary sector, in primary school and in the Foundation Stage it is far easier to identify and use the links, and, as noted in Chapter 7, the links can be expanded to cover much more than one subject area in addition to science, resulting in the planning and delivery of a cross-curricular topic. Putting science at the heart of a topic gives key learning and key skills across the curriculum a focus, and for the reluctant learner a real reason for engaging in the learning is provided. This can be illustrated by the details of a cross-curricular topic inspired by football.

The football ground

The cross-curricular topic would begin with a visit to a local football team's ground. The visit may include one or more of the following, depending on the football ground chosen:

- walking around the ground;

- having a conducted tour by the ground staff;
- visiting the gift shop;
- watching a practice session;
- involvement in training with the staff and/or community players;
- attending a reserves' game;
- attending a full game.

The follow-up work in a range of subject areas may include some of the following ideas:

- *science* – investigating the effects of exercise on the body, investigating the diets of sportspeople, researching healthy eating choices and/or healthy lifestyle choices;
- *English* – reading biographies of the players, writing newspaper match reports, questioning a player;
- *maths* – estimating and measuring the size of pitch using standard and non-standard measures, making a scale model of the pitch, carrying out calculations using money (based on prices in the gift shop);
- *design and technology* – evaluating a range of football boots, designing a new-style football boot;
- *geography* – using atlases to locate the countries of the foreign players in the squad;
- *history* – researching a time-line of the club visited;
- *art* – making portraits of players in different media, montages of different areas of the football ground;
- *PE* – using warm-up exercises the players use, providing the data for the scientific investigation into the effects of exercise on the body, developing knowledge about the rules of football in theory and in practice.

It can be seen that each subject area has some part to play in the whole topic, providing a full picture of the football ground visited. For the reluctant learner there is a reason for each of the skills used and the learning presented. It is a motivational topic, as almost all pupils are interested to some degree in sport. The sporting theme could be changed, so that rugby, athletics or the Olympics becomes the focus; it really depends on your interests and those of your pupils.

Planning checklist

Within the football-ground example of cross-curricular planning, I have not included music, religious education or ICT, and yet activities in these areas can also be identified: the use of music to convey feelings, e.g. the theme music to sporting programmes on television; the religions of the players and why their religion is important to them; and the use of ICT to research information about football, to find out about the league the team plays in or evaluating the team's website. However, it is important when planning a cross-curricular topic not to try to include all subject areas unless there is a natural link to the topic theme. This was one of the criticisms of topic work of the past – that contrived links were looked for at the expense of planning a challenging topic that provided progression in learning in all subject areas. Therefore, when planning for cross-curricular work it is too simplistic merely to identify a set of linked activities as I have presented above. What is needed is for the teacher to assess the next stage in the pupils' learning in each curriculum area and to plan a topic whereby the objectives for each subject area may be linked to one central theme. The brief checklist for effective cross-curricular planning given in Chapter 7 can be used by the teacher to ensure that the cross-curricular topic is planned so as to be challenging for all pupils and ensures progression in learning in all the subject areas covered.

- *The topic is well thought out* – the teacher considers the learning needed across the curriculum and identifies objectives for each subject area.
- *The topic is well planned* – the teacher takes the objectives, identifies and looks for common links and then identifies a topic focus.
- *The topic is structured* – using the plan, the teacher plans the order of the activities in order to build on the learning across the subjects linked.
- *The topic is based on common themes, skills and understandings* – the teacher identifies common themes, skills and under-standings that will be used and/or consolidated during the topic work.
- *The topic focus links together appropriate subject areas* – only

subject areas that naturally fit into the topic are linked; contrived links are avoided.

- *The topic work retains and emphasizes the individuality of each subject area* – the pupils are aware of the subject being studied, and the lesson objective relates to development in the identified subject.

The checklist is purely a planning aid for the teacher to ensure that the topic is relevant to the pupils' learning needs and is not simply used to motivate reluctant learners into engaging in learning for learning's sake. Although there may be times when activities are presented to pupils merely to interest them in the curriculum, the overriding purpose for using a cross-curricular topic is to motivate reluctant learners to progress in their learning. It is therefore vital for the teacher to become familiar with this checklist and to ensure that progression in learning takes place. Indeed, the lack of challenge and lack of progression in learning is one of the reasons why learners may become reluctant to engage in the curriculum being offered.

'A Victorian Washday'

Scientific enquiry within a topic on the theme of the Victorians that I have planned and carried out with a Year 5 class certainly fulfilled all the criteria set out above for effective planning for cross-curricular work.

- I thought through the topic I was proposing and the opportunities in a range of subject areas that the topic could provide.
- The topic was well planned, as I considered the learning needed at this stage by the majority of pupils and identified relevant activities to deliver the learning.
- I thought through the order of the work, to give the topic structure and to ensure that each activity carried out built on the learning across the subjects linked.
- I identified common links between subject areas – themes, skills and understandings.
- I identified objectives for each subject area that could naturally be linked to the topic theme.

- The pupils were made aware throughout the topic which subject was being studied; I ensured that they were made aware of the learning to take place within each activity by sharing the learning objective with them at the start of each lesson.

The pupils and I followed up the initial introduction to life in Victorian times by turning the classroom into a Victorian classroom for a day. The furniture was arranged in rows, we wore typical Victorian dress and followed a typical day's lessons: copywriting, learning by rote and drill exercises. We addressed each other appropriately and the pupils rose to their feet whenever an adult entered the room. This gave the pupils a real feel for school life Victorian-style.

Next we had a Victorian washday in the school yard. The pupils were introduced to the Victorian equipment for washing: dolly and tub, ponch and washboard. Each pupil had a go, and so the washing took all day. The pupils then compared a modern washday to a Victorian washday, focusing on the equipment used and the time taken to wash and dry the clothes.

The scientific enquiry was to compare the block soap used by the Victorians and modern-day washing powder. The whole class discussed how the comparison could be made. The final plan involved the following:

- Using a cotton fabric for washing.
- Using damp soil, tomato ketchup and felt-tip pen to soil the fabric.
- Testing bar soap similar to that the Victorians used, washing powder and liquid travel wash.
- Factors to be kept the same were identified: size of fabric, amount of soap/powder/travel wash, temperature of water, amount of water, length of time in the water, amount of agitation, number of times rinsed.
- One piece of fabric to be washed in plain water – as a control.
- All fabric to be dried naturally after washing and rinsing – by pegging it out on a washing line.

The scientific enquiry followed on naturally from the historical enquiry the pupils were engaged in. It was a *real* investigation carried out for a *real* purpose. The pupils were fully motivated and really wanted to know the outcome of the test. They drew heavily on their knowledge of the skills of scientific enquiry and formulated an investigation plan that they knew would result in a fair test. They understood the need for a control in the investigation – the washing in plain water to identify which stains could be removed without soap or washing powder. The investigation was to be carried out in groups, and each group was eager to adhere to the overall plan so that the various sets of results could be compared.

Of the three products being tested, it was concluded that the travel wash was the best product for cleaning stained clothes, as the fabric came out the brightest colour and even the felt-tip pen stain had been removed, although some of the soil stain remained. None of the products cleaned the fabric completely. The pupils suggested that further tests could compare the products in different temperatures of water and test them in a washing machine.

As an aside to the investigation, the following day a parent came in to ask the exact name of the travel wash we had tested, as her child had recounted the test to her and she had never successfully removed felt-tip pen stains from her children's clothes before. Although I usually relate this as an amusing anecdote, it did demonstrate that the child had been sufficiently enthused by the science work to discuss it at home, and the parent had sufficient faith in our results to ask the name of the product.

Science and ICT

ICT is a powerful tool to use across the whole curriculum. Pupils are increasingly enthusiastic and proficient users of information technology, with the majority now having access to some form of ICT in the home. Not only is ICT motivational for the learner but it also provides excellent links to teaching and learning for all the reasons given earlier for linking science to other subjects. The use of ICT within science offers considerable potential for enriching and enhancing the science curriculum, through the provision of opportunities for interactive learning and the presentation of work. The use of ICT within science is limited only by the teacher's and the pupils' imaginations, although the golden rule with ICT is only to use it when it is the best method for the task being carried out. Again I present a top ten list of appropriate uses for ICT within science.

1. researching information using the Internet;
2. information gathering using CD-ROMs;
3. developing knowledge and understanding through the use of scientific simulations;
4. observing natural phenomena such as space, weather changes and the like, viewed over the Internet;
5. data-logging equipment to record changes in light, changes in temperature over time, etc.;
6. presenting results of investigations using a graphing package;
7. use of a digital camera to record observations, changes over time, etc.;
8. use of a digital microscope to record observations – for example, the movements of a water shrimp;
9. using e-mail, perhaps to ask questions of scientists, or to report findings in science to an audience;
10. using a presentation package to present knowledge and understanding.

The use of ICT across the whole curriculum has grown phenomenally in recent years. It is usual now for schools to have a dedicated ICT suite together with one or more computers in each classroom. The usage of ICT must therefore be carefully planned for within the science lesson. Again the learning objective indicates whether a lesson is focusing on development in ICT capability, with science providing the context, or is focusing on development in science, with ICT skills being used as a vehicle for the learning. As before, the use of ICT must complement the learning process and provide progression in the learning taking place.

The use of ICT must not be thought of only in terms of the computer, Internet access and CD-ROMs, as audiovisual materials and equipment are also resources that come under the umbrella term of ICT. These include:

- audio tape recorders;
- radio;
- videos and DVDs;
- digital cameras;
- digital videos;
- digital microscopes.

These are important resources in ICT and must not be forgotten when one is planning to use ICT within science; recording work using a digital video and then making a DVD is a powerful means for engaging even the most reluctant of learners. It can be appreciated that this type of activity may have a scientific focus or an ICT focus, that the skills of using the recorder are enhancing the scientific work being carried out or that science is being used as a context for acquiring the skills needed to use the digital video.

The ICT area

It is worth giving thought here to the ICT area in the classroom, as the use of ICT may provide problems of access for the pupil that may, in turn, deter reluctant learners. An effective ICT area will have the following features:

- a designated space in the classroom;
- all ICT equipment stored appropriately;
- a range of software, relevant to the current learning taking place, on display or stored alongside the computer;
- age-appropriate information the pupils may need in order to use the software effectively;
- relevant website addresses on display and book-marked on the computer;
- support equipment stored in the area, e.g. spare batteries for the digital camera; blank disks;
- support materials, such as note-taking materials and question boards.

Using ICT in teaching

ICT is not only a subject for pupils to study, but also a valuable teaching resource that enables the teacher to produce quality teaching materials for encouraging all learners, including the more reluctant ones. Accordingly, teachers use ICT as a teaching resource in a variety of ways:

- accessing information from the Internet and CD-ROMs;
- downloading lesson plans from the Internet;
- writing lesson plans;
- making resources, e.g. scientific games;
- accessing professional support from websites aimed at teachers;
- making worksheets: partly completed printed sheets designed for the pupil to complete;
- making work cards: laminated cards for presenting instructions or for recording observations during an activity, using a wipe-on, wipe-off pen.

Using ICT to produce teaching materials can be particularly motivating for the reluctant learner because of the quality of the resource that can be generated. Text and pictures or photographs are easily combined, together with eye-catching and pleasing layouts and overall designs. However, even though worksheets and work cards may be used very effectively, it is worth considering the following.

- Although a high-quality work card or worksheet may be motivational, it is not guaranteed to be!
- Thought must be given to the intended learning before the work card or worksheet is produced.
- Poorly thought out sheets will be counter-productive so far as learning is concerned.
- An over-reliance on commercial worksheets may also be counter-productive to learning, owing to the likelihood of frustration and boredom setting in for reluctant learners.
- Reliance on worksheets may inhibit the pupils' responses.
- Reliance on worksheets may lead to lower standards of attainment.
- Worksheets and work cards must never be used merely to *occupy* pupils; any learning taking place will be meaningless.
- Quality interactions between pupil and teacher, between pupil and pupil, and between pupil and equipment are still

required even with the most motivational work card or worksheet.

Science and the Internet

The consideration of the relationship between science and ICT in the previous section has touched on the use of the Internet, but its importance warrants a section of its own. The impact of the Internet on science teaching and learning cannot be over-estimated, and it has a particular role to play within all the subject combinations noted earlier, and in the development of key skills.

The Internet has now become so commonplace and widely used that almost all pupils are confident in surfing the web and accessing a plethora of information. I have found that even the most reluctant of learners will engage in tasks that involve using the Internet in some way. However, when using the Internet with pupils it is imperative that safety is considered first. Appropriate safety measures include:

- the use of child-friendly search engines only e.g. www.ask-jeeves.co.uk, www.yahooligans.com;
- older pupils being allowed to use an appropriate search engine to find information;
- for younger pupils, it is preferable that sites to be used by the pupils are visited first by the teacher and then bookmarked for use by the pupils;
- not allowing discussion in chatrooms;
- not allowing the giving of personal information over the Internet.

Once these safety measures are in place, the Internet can be successfully used for researching information; for observing natural phenomena, for example the weather changing over time in different areas of the globe; for observing scientific moments of the past, for example the space programme; and/or to introduce a topic or an investigation to be carried out. In the next section I provide my top ten list of free websites for use with pupils of all ages, although this list changes almost daily as I discover new sites and sources of information. Alongside each web address I have explained why the site is in my top ten at the present time. These are all sites that may be used with pupils; my top ten list of sites for teachers is given in Appendix 2.

Top ten websites for pupils

1. *www.ask.co.uk* – a particularly child-friendly search engine that I also use often when searching for basic information. It is the *ask jeeves* web address.
2. *www.nasa.gov* – the home page for the NASA space programme. Pupils are able to search for information about space, download pictures or watch a video clip from a space exploration.
3. *www.nhm.ac.uk/education* – this is the web site of the Natural History Museum in London. As well as providing information of interest, it enables pupils to take part in online investigations.
4. *www.shu.ac.uk/schools/sci/sol/contents.htm* – this web site, supported by Sheffield Hallam University, is full of information and links to other web sites so that its uses are almost endless. There are four main sections, three for pupils and one for teachers – the prep room. The areas for pupils are the library for information, the science café for chatting to scientists and the lab for investigating.
5. *www.sciencemuseum.org.uk/learning/student/index.asp* – the student area of the Science Museum in London. Another site packed with information, ideas for investigations and video clips.
6. *www.planet-science.com* – the website started in 2001 as part of the Department for Education and Skills Science Year project, after which it was renamed Planet Science. The site again is packed with information, ideas and investigations to motivate the most reluctant of learners.
7. *http://insideout.rigb.org/ri/index.jsp* – from the Royal Institution of Great Britain. The site includes information and games, and suggests why science is important to us.
8. *www.spartechsoftware.com/reeko* – this web site offers a source of many science investigations and facts. It also invites pupils to contact Reeko the Scientist with questions or comments.

9. *www.the-ba.net* – the web site of the British Association for the Advancement of Science, containing news items and information about current issues.

10. *www.dctech.com/eureka* – this site has a small selection of stories about real scientists and their work. There are also online puzzles and activities to carry out.

One further site I'd recommend at this time for older pupils is www.channel4.com/sos – the *SOS* standing for Secondary Online Science. This site is aimed at 11- to 14-year-olds and presents help with science through the playing of games and through quizzes. I've not yet used the site with my pupils, but it does appear to be an inviting site for the age group targeted and for the more able primary-aged pupil.

All the web sites are important resources as they provide inspiration for pupils to research further or investigate further. I enjoy following the links to other pages, ideas and other web sites, and find that the ideas presented are merely starting points for other relevant science work.

Science beyond the classroom

Science is all around us; indeed, that is the point of science! It is not just the application of science, the medical advances, the space exploration, the technological advances that are important to our everyday lives but what is outside the classroom. Restricting scientific study to the classroom is denying our pupils the opportunity to experience science at first hand in the environment and in the workplace. The study of plants and animals in their natural habitats by observing them outside the confines of the classroom is far preferable to, and far more real than, using books or the computer. Science is the study of *what is* and *why it is*, and therefore, whenever possible, should be studied *where it is*. Experiencing science at first hand is far more motivational for reluctant learners than the highest-quality teaching materials the teacher can make. Science beyond the classroom has been covered in Chapter 3 and 4. Among other places, it can be carried out in:

- the school grounds;
- the locality;

- local businesses and industry – many local businesses will accommodate school visits if you are able to detail exactly what you want your pupils to see and experience;
- museums and libraries;
- parks and wildlife centres;
- shops;
- countryside areas;
- coastal areas.

Again it is only the limits to the teacher's imagination and creativity that restrict the study of science beyond the classroom. Visits to science centres are an excellent starting point for the teacher in building up a list of relevant places to visit; the ideas contained within them often suggest other places to the teacher. For example, exhibits about lenses may lead to a visit to the local optician's, or an exhibition on forces may lead to a visit to the local park to observe forces in action at the adventure playground. These activities will provide real meaning to the learners and therefore allow them to progress in their knowledge, understanding and attitudes.

I have enjoyed many, many visits with my pupils. In addition to the ones listed throughout the book, others that I have enjoyed (and my pupils enjoyed!) include visits to:

- a local supermarket – to see bread being made;
- a garden centre and pet shop – to learn about the conditions needed to grow plants and to keep animals;
- a country park – to observe creatures in their natural habitat;
- the theatre – to learn about light and sound and the effects that can be produced;
- the local secondary school – to use its weather station;
- the printers of a local newspaper – to find out about different papers and the inks used.

'Science and Fast Food'

Within walking distance of the school where I teach is a fast-food restaurant that the pupils often use. They are therefore familiar with the venue and are comfortable visiting it. A class visit informed the pupils of the part science played in the restaurant and formed the basis for an excellent cross-curricular topic.

During the visit the pupils were given a conducted tour of the food stores and food preparation areas. They (and I) were fascinated by the method for making soft drinks, providing a real-life context for understanding the properties of liquids and gases, backed up by the properties of solids and the processes of freezing and melting when considering the use of the freezers. The pupils observed meal orders being taken and meals prepared and cooked and then served to customers. They developed an understanding not only of the part science played in the restaurant but also of the extensive use of technology. The visit placed the study of the properties of the three states of matter in context they were familiar with, and focused on reversible and irreversible changes in the kitchen.

Other work during the visit consisted of:

- reading signs, menus and information (literacy);
- data collection (numeracy);
- evaluating logos, evaluating packaging and labelling of products, evaluating products (design and technology);
- reviewing the location of the restaurant (geography);
- field-sketches (art).

This was followed up by work in the classroom concentrating on:

- report writing, poetry writing, persuasive posters and advertising and research skills (literacy);
- word problems involving money, data handling, graphing (numeracy);
- designing logos, designing and making a new food product, designing and making packaging and labelling of the product (design and technology);
- researching relevant information, data handling, presenting ideas (ICT);
- use of land space (geography);
- recreating packaging design, montages of packages (art);
- evaluating radio jingles, writing own radio jingles (music).

The visit was important to the topic because it set the topic in focus and used a context familiar to the pupils but looked at it in different ways from those they were used to. It provided a real-life context for their explorations, again providing a purpose for the learning, and was therefore motivating the pupils. The subjects linked had natural connections and led to developments in the pupils' learning across the subjects. The common skills used included:

- pupils finding out information for themselves;
- using different senses to gather information;
- using the skills of exploration, questioning and consulting others;
- hypothesizing – why the restaurant was sited where it was, why people used the restaurant;
- suggesting possible solutions to problems – fulfilling all customer needs;
- participating in group discussions;
- listening to the views and ideas of others;
- commenting on others' ideas;
- initiating interactions with adults as information sources;
- using secondary sources of information.

Part Four

Troubleshooting

10 Recognizing and assessing attainment in science

It is not enough merely to engage the reluctant learner in science and scientific study, through the exciting range of activities we can provide; the science curriculum must promote learning for *all* pupils, in order for them to progress in the acquisition of knowledge, skills, understandings of science and scientific attitudes. In order to ensure this progression in learning, it is essential that teachers:

- are able to recognize the achievements of their pupils;
- know the subsequent stages in learning;
- are able to plan a programme of developmental activities leading to the next stage of learning;
- assess the pupils' progress towards the next stage of learning.

This list describes the basis of target setting: identifying where the pupils are now in terms of their attainment, setting a target for where they should be in their learning at the end of a set period of time, and then breaking that overall target down into short-term objectives that build upon each other to ensure that the learners meet the overall target set, and assessing the pupils throughout to map their progress through the science curriculum. It can be appreciated how important assessment is for recognizing attainment in science at different stages and how the assessment data contribute to the target-setting process. This part of the book is therefore concerned with strategies for recognizing attainment in science through an overview of assessment procedures that may be used, both day-to-day assessments and assessments carried out at the end of a period of related study, whereas the cycle of target setting will be looked at in more detail in Chapter 17.

It is important that assessment is considered a basic tool that the teacher uses within teaching and learning, a tool that provides vital information regarding a pupil's learning in science. Assessment is not a process that ends after the information has been collected; its usefulness is in how this information is used in ways that are important for teaching and learning. Assessment information is used for numerous purposes, including:

- indicating the areas in which the pupil is progressing in science;
- identifying the learning needs of the pupil;
- identifying misconceptions in science;
- providing feedback to the pupil on his or her progress;
- feeding the next stages in planning;
- setting future targets for the pupil's learning;
- identifying short-term targets for the pupil;
- identifying how the pupil approached the task;
- identifying difficulties – both general to the curriculum and specific to science;
- identifying the need for support for future learning, such as the use of scaffolding for recording science, or working with an adult to ensure that tasks are understood, for example.

There are other benefits to assessment, but perhaps the most important one for reluctant learners is the enhanced motivation it can lead to. The enhanced motivation it generates may be due to the pupils having a fuller understanding of what they have achieved in science, to the pupils having a greater knowledge about what they need to achieve next in their learning, or to the welcome increase in adult attention they receive throughout the assessment period. The results of assessment may aid in raising reluctant learners' self-esteem by using assessment evidence to demonstrate the strides they are making in their learning, and the extra attention they receive may be particularly motivational. It is therefore imperative for these learners to be a part of the assessment process.

What to assess

Assessments take many forms, from informally noting how a pupil responds to a given activity, to an end-of-topic *test*. It can be appreciated that different assessments are needed for different purposes, such as the purposes outlined earlier in this chapter. In addition, it is important to assess pupils' attainment in science as a whole and not to concentrate solely on factual knowledge or the understanding of scientific concepts. The following strands must all therefore be assessed:

- scientific skills – the ability to use the skills in practice, knowing how and when to use the skills;
- scientific knowledge – being able to recall facts, such as the order of the planets in the solar system;
- scientific understanding – the ability to apply knowledge in a new situation, e.g. applying the processes of evaporation and condensation to a problem that can be solved using evaporation;
- scientific attitudes – the demonstration of attitudes towards science study, e.g. curiosity, empathy.

In assessing these strands, it is important that there is a balance between *what* is assessed and *how* it is assessed. Teachers must develop a range of strategies for collecting valid assessment evidence for all their pupils – evidence that truly reflects the pupils' attainment in science. Having valid evidence is vital for assessment to be used effectively to promote further learning, an essential requirement for all pupils but particularly for reluctant learners. As noted throughout the book, there may be many reasons why learners become reluctant or disengaged from their learning, but two particular types of pupil who can be addressed through the effective use of assessment are the gifted pupil who should be a high attainer but is bored by the level of science work on offer, and the pupil with low self-esteem, who may be further encouraged by knowing his or her level of attainment. Both these categories of reluctant learner will be considered within this part of the book and in Part Five, 'Science for All'.

Forms of assessment

Assessment may be very simple or very complex! At its simplest there are just two forms of assessment: assessment *for* learning and assessment *of* learning. These replace formative and summative assessments. Assessment *for* learning is the term for the ongoing daily assessments that influence planning, whereas assessment *of* learning is the assessment made at the end of a period of teaching and learning that measures the learning that has taken place. At its most complex, assessment is considered in terms of being formal, informal, diagnostic, formative, summative, criterion referenced, norm referenced or evaluative, but the boundaries between the different forms are not always clearly defined. It is even possible for an assessment to involve a number of forms at the same time. For example, a single assessment may be classed as criterion referenced, formative and informal! For the purposes of this book it is the use of assessment that is important, and how this impacts on the reluctant learner, rather than the need to be able to identify each type of assessment used, and so I will only briefly outline each of these assessment types:

- *Formal assessment* – an assessment that is planned in advance, has an intended framework, occurs at a specified time and is formally recorded.
- *Informal assessment* – all teachers carry out informal assessments continually – for example, through observation and discussions with pupils. These assessments are most valuable for aiding pupils in their work as it is occurring.
- *Diagnostic assessment* – made by the teacher to analyse and classify learning and learning difficulties, so that appropriate assistance and interventions can take place.
- *Formative assessment* – ongoing, everyday assessment used to identify achievements made by a pupil, to establish where the pupil has progressed to, how these achievements can be built on and the next steps to be taken.
- *Summative assessment* – an assessment made at the end of a period of teaching: the end of a topic or unit of work, the end of a term, end of a year or end of a key stage. The results of these assessments are used by subsequent teachers of the child, by the whole school, by a child's subsequent school (in the case of transition) and as a basis for a formal report to the parents.
- *Criterion-referenced assessment* – an assessment that assesses a pupil's achievement against an agreed set of standards or

competences, such as the level descriptions for science within the National Curriculum Order.

- *Norm-referenced assessment* – an assessment that compares the achievement of one pupil with the achievements of others. The *norms* therefore describe the average or typical performance in that assessment and for that assessment group only. (Norm-referenced assessment differs from criterion-referenced in that the standards to be attained are not necessarily dictated by external documentation, such as the National Curriculum, but are dictated by the particular group of pupils being assessed.)
- *Evaluative assessment* – an assessment that is used to appraise and influence school policies and planning on a wider scale than the planning by individual teachers only. Evaluative assessment may be used to determine the effectiveness of the school policy and scheme of work for science, to measure the breadth and balance of the science curriculum and to ensure progression and continuity in pupils' learning in science.

Although for the purposes of this book it is not important to know and understand all the different forms of assessment, it is important for the teacher to use a range of assessments over the course of a period of teaching. To aid assessment for learning, the ongoing, everyday assessments and the setting of lesson objectives, detailing the exact learning to take place, are essential for the teacher to be able to assess the learning that has taken place throughout the lesson. Here the teacher may use informal assessments that are criterion referenced – that is, related to expected attainment for the age group taught – or norm referenced – that is, comparing the individual pupil's attainment to that of the group as a whole. These assessments will be formative, as they will influence further teaching, and may be diagnostic in that any pupils experiencing difficulties may be identified and the future teaching amended to cater for the needs of those pupils. It is also through this type of assessment that the needs of reluctant learners may be identified, leading to a more appropriate curriculum or style of delivery for such pupils.

In addition to the ongoing formative assessments, the

assessments of learning, the use of formal, summative assessments at the end of a period of teaching is needed in order to judge the development of knowledge, skills, understandings and/or attitudes over the period of teaching. The summative assessments may also be evaluative in that the appropriateness of the work presented to the pupils may be assessed, possibly leading to changes in the school's policy and/or practices. The most formal of all summative assessments, which are also evaluative, are of course the end-of-key stage SATs for science, and science-based GCSEs.

Approaching assessment

Assessment is therefore to be considered merely a tool for the teacher to use – to identify attainment, to indicate further learning needs, leading to increased engagement in the science curriculum, and then to further attainment for all pupils, including the reluctant learners. It is not an end in itself but is most valuable for ensuring that the science work on offer is appropriate, challenging and accessible while being exciting, relevant and inspiring. All assessments therefore have purpose, and so, when approaching assessment, teachers need to consider *why* they are assessing, *what* they are assessing and *how* they will assess. The following questions will aid teachers in being clear about the assessment purpose and in deciding on the form of assessment and the strategy they will use. The main questions to be asked are:

- What information do I need?
- Why do I need this information?
- How may this information be collected?
- How will I know the information is valid?

Only when these questions have been answered can the form of assessment be considered, although this process of identification does not include the informal, unplanned assessments that teachers carry out almost all the time. These informal, unplanned assessments include spontaneous observations, comments to pupils regarding their work or engagement in the task, and questions to pupils about the activity being conducted. Often, because it is spontaneous and relaxed, this type of assessment yields unexpected and unanticipated information that is very informative regarding the learning. Over an extended period of time, this type of assessment is essential for providing a wide-ranging evidence base, including the identification of learning needs within science, and so it is important to record these observations in some way. This recording of observations will be considered in more detail later in this chapter and in Chapter 17.

The questions specified above are necessary for identifying the scope of the assessment required, without the need to refer to the terminology of assessment. Using the questions, the teacher is identifying:

- the information needed from the assessment – for example, information about the application of a skill or the understanding of a concept;
- the purpose of the information to be collected – for example, to inform future planning, to identify individual needs, to evaluate his or her teaching;
- the strategy for assessment to be used – for example, observation, or formal test;
- the basis for knowing the assessment has provided a true picture – that is, answering the question, 'how do I know how well the pupil is achieving?'.

These questions are essential when planning for assessment, as within any lesson or teaching activity pupils will be demonstrating a range of skills, knowledge, understandings and attitudes; not all can be assessed during one teaching session! The questions will therefore focus teachers on what information they require and how this information will be collected. *How* the information is collected indicates the strategy to be used – and there are many, many strategies that teachers regularly employ. It is worth looking here at some of the main strategies used, before considering the basis for determining the validity of the assessments made.

Observation

As has already been noted, classroom observations are carried out continuously throughout the day; all teachers develop this skill and carry out observations almost without realizing it! These assessments, albeit unplanned and informal, may yield a vast amount of information regarding the pupils' progress within the lesson and provide a continuous assessment of children's knowledge, skills, understandings and attitudes. However, often these informal assessments, together with some questioning at the beginning and end of a lesson, may be used solely to judge the success of the lesson rather than to assess an individual pupil's progress. It is therefore important for the teacher to note such assessments and to make use of the information and evidence they provide. They are particularly valuable for noting the needs of the reluctant learners. They may aid teachers in recognizing a pattern in reluctant learners' engagement with the curriculum. For example, are they more engaged with investigative work than with other types of work? Are they more engaged in open-ended tasks than the shorter, more focused tasks? Are they obviously put off when writing is involved? By identifying a pattern, you can cater for reluctant learners' needs by relying more on the activities they do engage in and by providing extra support for activities where they are more liable to become disengaged from the learning.

Classroom observations are also a fundamental source of information in identifying and diagnosing learning difficulties, and again may be used to monitor progress over time, to provide an insight into the ways in which a particular pupil learns and works, thus enabling the teacher to plan an appropriate curriculum delivery that incorporates the support needed by the pupil. (The planning of appropriate curriculum delivery will be looked at in more detail in Part Five of this book.)

Classroom observation is also a particularly valuable strategy for collecting information or evidence where:

- the scientific work being carried out will not produce a piece of retainable evidence or it is inappropriate to ask pupils to record their work on paper;
- the evidence cannot be paper based – for example, the way in which a pupil approaches an activity, the way the pupil interacts within a group carrying out a task;
- the evidence can only be shared orally with the teacher – for example, the thought process the pupil goes through when approaching a task.

Because of its importance in providing assessment evidence, observation should not always be an unplanned, almost passive strategy that the teacher uses. It is also an active process that is planned carefully, is focused and carried out thoroughly. When you are planning to assess through observation, the following checklist may be used to ensure both that the observation process is thought through carefully and that it will, in turn, yield the assessment evidence required.

- *What is being observed?* It is important that observations focus on one manageable objective or set of objectives and that the observations to be made are identified. For example, will the children's actions be observed, or conversations or presentations of work recorded?
- *Who will be observed?* Do not try to collect assessment evidence for large numbers of children simultaneously through observation; focus on one small group within the lesson.
- *Where will the observer sit or stand during the observation?* Will you position yourself near the group, to ensure an overview of all the members of the group, or will you sit next to two identified pupils?
- *Will the observer be with the pupils he or she is observing all through the lesson, or at intervals?* Is it necessary for the observer to stay with the group throughout the lesson or will observing at intervals generate sufficient assessment evidence? If observing at intervals, have these been planned in advance? Will the observations take place at regular intervals throughout the activity or at fixed points throughout the activity? Do you need to visit each pupil in the group in turn or the group as a whole? Ensure that there will be sufficient time during each of the planned observations to gather the necessary information required.
- *Who will carry out the observation?* Does it always have to be the teacher who carries out the observations? Teachers and support staff need to develop the skills of observation, particularly where the observations are unplanned, and so planned observations will aid in the acquisition of the skills needed. Under the guidance of the teacher, therefore, support staff will be able to focus on these skills and develop

their ability to make observations and to talk to groups of pupils and individuals.

- *What will the observer's role be?* It is important that the observer is clear about the amount of his or her involvement with the task, and how this will affect the assessments made.
- *Against what criteria will the learning be being assessed?* For example, you might want to assess it against a particular aspect of the National Curriculum.
- *What further information, and from what source, will reinforce the assessments made through the observation?* This may include a discussion with a pupil or group of pupils, the marking of written work or the results of a formal test.
- *Are the children to be made aware of the purposes of the observation?* An explanation of what is being observed may enable the pupils to demonstrate more readily what they know or what they can do. For reluctant learners an unexplained yet formal observation may intimidate them and not provide the opportunity for them to accurately demonstrate their learning.
- *How will I interpret my observations of actions and behaviour?* Having observed the pupils, what information have you obtained regarding the pupils' progress in science?
- *What roles will careful questioning and discussion play in the observation?* Discussion with pupils is a crucial aspect of classroom observation in that the pupils are able to explain their successes, their difficulties, their understandings, etc.
- *How will the observations and/or conversations be recorded?* Is a standard format needed or will notes be taken and retained in some form?
- *How will I ensure that all pupils are on task during an observation?* What strategies will be employed to enable the observer to concentrate on the small group or individuals being assessed while catering for the needs of the rest of the class, ensuring that interruptions are limited?

Marking work

Although not all science work results in a piece of recorded work, there are a number of ways in which pupils may record their explorations and investigations in science. These include:

- pieces of writing;
- models;
- drawings;
- paintings;
- tables;
- charts;
- posters;
- ICT work.

Each recorded outcome may be used to assess the extent of a pupil's learning against the lesson objective, a National Curriculum level description or part of a level description, or a stepping stone towards an Early Learning Goal. A collection of such pieces of work can illustrate a pupil's attainment over time; it may also be used as a benchmark for the assessment of others, by providing an exemplar set of work at the level expected from a particular group of pupils. The use of such a collection of work in motivating learners will be looked at in more detail in Chapter 17, whereas marking and feedback will be looked at in Chapter 11.

Although marking and assessing pupil outcomes may result in a judgement about attainment, it is preferable to assess the outcome in conjunction with the assessments made during classroom observation and/or through discussion, as concrete products alone may not provide sufficient or conclusive evidence of attainment. The use of marking of recorded work may produce assessment information that is incomplete because the work does not truly reflect the pupil's knowledge and understanding; the pupil's attainment in science may be masked by difficulties with English, mathematics or art; or it may be difficult to match the features of the piece of work to the learning intended. It is therefore imperative that the marked work is only a part of the overall assessment. Marked work may only stand as a complete piece of assessment evidence if it is the summative assessment made at the end of a period of teaching.

Discussion

Throughout the consideration of using classroom observations and/or marked work, the need to supplement the assessment evidence with discussion with the pupil was noted. Discussion enables learners to demonstrate their learning and to articulate their ideas more fully, and allows the teacher to explore the pupils' ideas and developing knowledge, understandings and attitudes through careful questioning. Indeed, it is during discussion that the teacher is able to demonstrate his or her own effective questioning techniques! Careful questioning by the teacher is needed to support learners in sharing their learning and to explore the ideas given by the pupil, and so it is important for the teacher to develop a high-level questioning technique. Effective questions encourage pupils to talk through the thought processes they have gone through, and to explore the language of science discourse. Moreover, they ensure that pupils are fully able to demonstrate their understanding, knowledge and/or attitudes in science. However, the teacher must be mindful when carrying out a conversation with the pupil of the need to ensure that the questions posed appear *natural* rather than as questions to *test* the pupil. Some effective question openings include:

- What did you do when …?
- What happened when …?
- Why do you think … happened?
- When did something similar happen …?
- How can we …?
- What do you think this tells us about …?
- What could you …?
- I wonder if … always happens like this?

As with observation, the use of effective questioning is to be carefully planned by the teacher, especially when using it within a discussion with reluctant learners. A reluctant learner may demonstrate his or her disengagement with the curriculum by refusing to enter into a conversation with the teacher, by offering one-word answers or by offering an inappropriate answer. It is imperative that the teacher remain focused on the discussion and appear unflustered by the answers given, or by the silence that prevails. At this point it is at the discretion of the teacher whether to pursue the discussion, using careful questioning, or whether to abandon the discussion. However, it is a fact that the more interesting the topic is to learners, the more they are likely to engage in a discussion about the work. This is yet another indicator of the need to ensure that the science we offer is exciting, interesting, relevant and inspiring for all our learners.

A quiz

I often use quizzes with my classes, as all pupils seem to enjoy the elements of fun and winning! The presentation of questions as a quiz seems to motivate even the most reluctant of learners, and they willingly join in the fun. My quizzes are usually one half of the room versus the other, with points given for good answers and plenty of bonus points on offer – for supplementary questions, good ideas and appropriate teamwork. The knowledge and understanding demonstrated through these informal, unpressured sessions can be quite phenomenal and can lead to quite interesting discussions about the answers given. Pupils also enjoy writing their own quizzes, and again doing so can usefully demonstrate their knowledge and understanding. The pupils are asked to write a quiz, with answers, for use later in the day, without using a book to help them. This is an excellent technique to use with pupils if you don't want them to know you are assessing them, which can be important if the learners would be intimidated or constrained by the knowledge that their work was being assessed.

Assessment tasks

Assessment tasks are activities designed for the pupils to demonstrate their developing skills, knowledge, attitudes and understandings. The task may be a discussion about an event, a practical activity or investigation, or a question to answer at length. Tasks such as these, that are open-ended and open to interpretation by the pupils, are most useful for providing assessment evidence, as they may be completed individually, thereby giving a summative assessment of the pupils' learning. They may also be used with pairs or groups of pupils, in which case they offer opportunities for pupils to talk together, to share ideas, to question points being made and so to scaffold the learning being demonstrated. These opportunities for demon-strating shared learning are particularly important for pupils who are reluctant to engage in activities unaided or to carry out a one-to-one discussion with the teacher.

Formal testing

Inevitably, formal testing takes place throughout a pupil's school career. It is assessment *of* learning, and provides a summative assessment of what the pupil has learned, understands or *is able to do*. Formal tests are therefore often presented as closed tasks or questions and include SATs, public examinations and end-of-topic tests. The results may be used formatively for the pupils, in that they are used to amend future planning, but are designed to ascertain what the learner has learned, rather than to indicate where further learning needs to take place. The results are also used to make judgements about the quality of teaching, and consequently of the learning, taking place within an institution, and so are used to amend the curriculum if changes are indicated. It is important that all pupils, and in particular the reluctant learners, are prepared well for such tests, to ensure they are clear about how to approach the test, how to deal with time issues within the test and the range of answers that may be required. Although designed to find out the extent of the learning that has taken place, summative assessments should not inhibit the pupils and hinder their responses, through either the way in which they are presented to the pupils or the way in which the pupils access the tests. The assessment evidence from summative assessments is much less open to interpretation, as they are characterized by:

- closed questions requiring a one-word answer;
- ticking one of four statements;
- deciding whether a statement is *true* or *false*;
- short explanations of scientific models or theories;
- identifying errors in statements or diagrams.

Although it may be thought that this form of assessment is threatening to reluctant learners, in my experience it is a form they often appear to enjoy! They appreciate the simplicity of the answers required and the solitude the testing process brings. This is not true of all reluctant learners, of course, and so their needs, and the needs of all our pupils, must be considered fully. It is the role of the teacher to ensure that all the learners are prepared for these types of assessment and to provide support where needed, to ensure that the assessment evidence that is produced reflects the pupils' true attainment in science.

Recording assessment evidence

It is an important part of the assessment process to record the assessment evidence, as noted during the discussion about *classroom observations* on pp. 117–20. It is not appropriate for me to suggest ways in which this can be done, as most schools have a preferred style of recording and an agreed policy. Rather, I shall set out why such records are important to the teacher and to the learner.

Not all evidence is paper based, and even if it were, it would be unrealistic to make copies of all recorded outcomes, and yet records are an important reference source for:

- Referring back to throughout the course of a pupil's study – not only for this year's teacher but for teachers in future years.
- Planning the next steps in the pupil's learning – this is the overriding purpose of assessment.
- Demonstrating how the pupil's learning has progressed over time.
- Sharing information with the pupils – this is especially important where records of observations have been made, as the pupils may not have appreciated the learning they were demonstrating during the focused observation.
- To provide a set of exemplar materials for a particular level or age group of pupils. These may be used by teachers when levelling other work and for sharing with other pupils to demonstrate the standards and expectations for their own work. This may be particularly motivating for the reluctant learner to understand more clearly the outcomes needed.

It is therefore a matter of professional judgement, while being mindful of school policy, of what should be recorded. What is of overriding importance is that the records are clear, unambiguous, easy to interpret and of use to the class teacher and other staff within the school. This aspect of assessment will be looked at again in Chapter 17.

Interpreting assessment evidence

When assessment evidence has been collected, through observation, discussion, testing or a resulting piece of work, the evidence must be interpreted, in order to ascertain the attainment of the pupils and their progress towards the intended learning. First, the teacher must be clear about the intended learning and then be able to match the pupil outcome to that learning. Put simply, does the evidence indicate that the pupil has fully or partially met the objective set for the learning? When interpreting the evidence, you should also consider whether you have collected enough evidence to ensure that the pupil has demonstrated his or her true attainment. If not, you may have to make a reassessment or collect more evidence, perhaps using a different strategy. Some questions to consider here are:

- Did the assessment strategy or strategies allow the pupils to demonstrate the appropriate skills, knowledge, understandings and/or attitudes being assessed?
- Was the choice of assessment strategy, either as an integral part of teaching and learning or as a task, appropriate to the evidence to be collected?
- Did I make full use of open and closed questions during my discussion with the pupil?
- Do I assess the pupils regularly in my day-to-day teaching?
- Do I involve the pupils in assessing their own progress and achievements?
- Will I share the results of my assessments with the pupils?
- When, where and how will I share the results of my assessments with the pupils?
- Have I assessed all my pupils appropriately, including those with special needs, those for whom English is not their first language and the reluctant learners?

The evidence may be used at this stage to identify the next stage of learning to be planned and delivered, to determine the progress made towards the targets set for the pupil, to indicate further learning needs if the pupil has not met the learning objective or to measure the pupil's attainment against the requirements of the documentation for science. The next section looks at how attainment is measured against the documentation. The other uses of the evidence will be explored further in Chapter 17, within the requirements of target setting.

Levelling attainment

Within the National Curriculum Order for Science (Qualifications and Curriculum Authority 1999a) and the Early Learning Goals (Qualifications and Curriculum Authority 1999b) are statements against which the pupils' achievements are to be judged. For pupils aged 5 plus, these are the level descriptions indicating the range of knowledge, skills and understandings needed by pupils to be assigned a National Curriculum level of attainment. The level descriptions are the main standards used for criterion-referenced assessments prior to examinations at GCSE level. The given criteria within the level descriptions can also be very helpful for teachers when planning activities at an appropriate level for their pupils and for sharing the expected outcome of an activity with the pupils. The sharing of the requirements for different levels of attainment enables pupils to have a greater understanding of what is expected of them at different stages in their learning. It encourages them to take more responsibility for their own learning and clarifies what they need to do to be successful in their work and in the assessments. This can be particularly important for reluctant learners, who may not be engaged with learning until they understand both why they are carrying out an activity and what they need to achieve in order to demonstrate success. However, the statements made in the Early Learning Goals and the National Curriculum level descriptions for science are open to a certain amount of interpretation by the teacher, and so it is important for the teacher to be clear about the statements and what they look like in practice. A detailed outline of these statements is outside the scope of this book, but many teachers develop their understanding of the statements by working with their colleagues to moderate samples of work.

Samples of work are discussed with reference to the National Curriculum level descriptions, and common understandings of the statements are forged. What is most important in levelling work against the level description statements is the need to consider all the evidence provided, and to acknowledge all the sources of the evidence used, including notes and comments made during observations and discussions and assessment tasks. The evidence as a whole will therefore contribute to the judgements made; additional sources of evidence to acknowledge include photographs, songs, plays and presentations.

11 Marking and feedback

Marking and feedback are two further tools the teacher uses in teaching to inform pupils of how they are progressing in their learning. The processes may be used together, or feedback may be given without marking. They may be formal or informal processes; marking will follow the school's official policy and result in formal, written feedback, whereas informal feedback takes place within the normal exchanges between pupils and adults, with the teacher providing accurate, helpful and motivating feedback at appropriate times.

Pupils' work must always be marked carefully and accurately in order to provide written, practical feedback and for identifying where a pupil needs to go next to further his or her learning. Comments must always relate to the learning objective for the work, which will have been shared with the pupil at the start of the lesson. Relating comments to the learning objective ensures that the learners know what was expected of them during the lesson, what the intended outcome was and how near to meeting the learning objective they came. Thoughtfully marking a piece of work also demonstrates to the pupil that his or her work is of importance and is recognized by the teacher as being worthwhile. Whenever possible, it is preferable to mark a pupil's work with him or her, as the teacher can engage the pupil in a discussion about the work, particularly the strengths and the progress made towards the learning objective. This is particularly important when working with reluctant learners, who may need the teacher to identify for them where they have progressed in their learning.

All assessments that have been carried out, regardless of the strategy used to collect the assessment evidence, must result in pupils receiving feedback on their learning and their performance, again ensuring that assessment is a developmental activity and not an end in itself. By sharing our judgements with the pupils, we are helping them to work out how to improve and to increase their learning. Through feedback we are therefore using the judgements made through assessment to lead the pupils through a process of continuous improvement.

When marking a pupil's work, and then providing feedback to the pupil, the teacher is able once again to involve the learner in his or her own learning and in the assessment of that learning. The old adage that *nothing succeeds like success* is most certainly true, and so providing pupils with concrete examples of their progress, strengths (and weaknesses) can provide them with the confidence and interest needed to continue to achieve in science.

When providing feedback, written or verbal, it is important:

- to be positive in your comments;
- to provide at least one example of where the work shows progress from prior learning;
- to comment on work that is particularly pleasing;
- to ensure that the feedback supports the pupil in improving and developing knowledge, skills, understandings and/or attitudes;
- to use your comments to identify a target for the pupil to work on during future lessons, the *where next*;
- to comment on progress towards the learning objective;
- to praise publicly if appropriate, ensuring that all pupils know what it is you are praising.

Although feedback is an essential component of assessment and may be particularly motivating for reluctant learners who need constant approval and comments on their learning by the teacher, the teacher must also be wary of *feedback overload*. Feedback overload may demotivate rather than motivate certain reluctant learners, as they may feel it to be patronizing or worthless. For such pupils it may be more appropriate to give feedback at intervals, focusing on the progress made through a range of work rather than through individual pieces of work.

Identifying misconceptions

As I have noted many times in the book so far, assessment is not an end in itself, but an essential tool in identifying the next stages of learning and in identifying problems pupils may have accessing the science curriculum. One of the most interesting results of assessment is the identification of the misconceptions pupils hold in science. It is not surprising that pupils hold misconceptions in science, but they do not pose a problem to a pupil's progress in scientific knowledge and understanding if they are dealt with swiftly (in order for the pupil to build on his or her ideas) and sensitively (in order to maintain the self-esteem of the pupil). Pupils come to science with an understanding of science concepts of their own, built up over time. Indeed, even the youngest pupils enter school already holding many of their own ideas about natural phenomena, and so it is unsurprising that a range of misconceptions are held. The pupils then develop their ideas in science through the planned science curriculum you deliver, which builds on these ideas, and through a range of sources outside the school environment. What I find particularly interesting is that many pupils share the same misconceptions and that they may be extremely resistant to change. How easy it would be to simply instruct the pupil that their belief is wrong and then provide them with the correct ideas! In practice, the beliefs held by the pupil must be challenged systematically and developed through appropriate planned tasks and activities. Misconceptions should therefore not be viewed as the *wrong* ideas; they should be acknowledged as the present ideas and interpretations that fit the pupil's view of the world. Activities therefore need to be planned that:

- provide instances where the pupil notices differences in his or her own ideas and the evidence presented through investigation;
- encourage the pupil to discuss the differences;
- enable the pupil to test emerging ideas and theories;
- encourage the pupil to amend his or her ideas.

For all learners, including reluctant learners, it is imperative that their ideas are given value, in order for them to have the confidence to change those ideas. Activities that involve discussion following investigation, where all ideas are considered equally before being amended, are vital to ensure that the self-esteem of all pupils holding misconceptions is maintained or raised. The value of reflection and discussion in learning in science is considered both in Chapter 5 and in the following section.

Improving own learning and performance

The requirement for pupils to reflect on their work, to share their reflections with others and to use their reflections to develop and improve their own learning and performance is stated within the National Curriculum Order for Science (Qualifications and Curriculum Authority 1999a). I have already noted that reflection is essential for progress in science; it is also becoming increasingly a requirement across the curriculum and an essential part of assessment. It is therefore important that pupils are able to reflect critically on their own work and that of others, but for reluctant learners this can be a very difficult area to address. If a learner is reluctant because of low self-esteem, critical reflection can be a devastating requirement that further demotivates him or her. Yet again it is the teacher's sensitivity and appropriate planning that are needed to ensure that all learners develop the skills needed to be able to self-reflect. All learners need to be taught:

- to look back at their work and identify the positive features;
- to identify what they would change if they repeated the piece of work and why they would change it;
- to identify what they would they do in the same way and why they would do it the same way;
- to identify what they have learned through their work;
- to identify what they already knew that helped them with their work;
- to make a fair judgement about their progress in learning;
- to identify where they had problems in the learning, why they had problems and what they did to overcome the problems;
- to make suggestions regarding their future learning needs.

It must be noted that if all the above were carried out by each pupil after each activity, the rate of learning would reduce immediately! It is appropriate to plan for such evaluations to take place at certain points in a period of teaching and to focus on only one or two points under each area or to focus on one or two areas only. It can be appreciated that the teacher's role in self-evaluation is crucial. We are expecting pupils to self-reflect, but they do need guidance, coaching and information from the teacher in order to make sense of their learning and in order to plan the next steps in learning. The use of open yet focused questioning is essential yet again in this context, to enable pupils to identify correctly their own strengths and how to build on them and to acknowledge their weaknesses and identify how to deal with them. Pupils need information from the teacher regarding the learning expected and how this is able to progress; they are then in a position to work with the teacher to identify their own targets for future learning. The process of self-evaluation is also enhanced by quality feedback from the teacher during marking and feedback, as this models the procedure of reflection for the pupil.

This process provides the pupils with the opportunity to reflect not only on their own work but also on its relevance to them and the learning pathway they want to take. This ownership of the curriculum, albeit guided by the teacher at every stage, is crucial for the reluctant learners, to ensure that they have a reason to learn and have been involved in identifying the learning path they want to take.

Part Five

Science for All

12 Making science accessible and relevant to all pupils

It must almost go without saying that it is of major importance that through your teaching of science, all pupils are able to access a relevant and appropriate science curriculum. This is a fundamental responsibility of the teacher and embraces the notion of inclusion, the providing of effective learning opportunities for all pupils. Within the National Curriculum (www.nc.uk.net/nc_resources/html/inclusion) there is an inclusion statement regarding the provision of effective learning opportunities for all pupils, together with three principles for developing an inclusive curriculum. The three principles are:

- to set suitable learning challenges for all pupils;
- to respond to all pupils' learning needs;
- to overcome the potential barriers to learning for pupils.

These three principles have been considered throughout this book, particularly with respect to reluctant learners. This book is aimed at providing ideas for engaging reluctant learners in science through the provision of a relevant, exciting, interesting and inspiring curriculum, and how such a curriculum can be used to overcome reluctant learners' barriers to learning. The need to address the learners' needs has been touched on throughout and will be looked at in more detail here.

It is here that your understanding of equal opportunities in science must be explored – your response to providing equality of opportunity in science and how you provide for this within your teaching. Equality of opportunity relates not only to the two main areas of diversity – multi-culture and gender – but to gifted and talented pupils, reluctant learners, the less able, and pupils with recognized special needs. It can be appreciated from the phrase itself, *equality of opportunity*, that providing equal opportunities in the classroom does not mean treating all pupils in the same way, but is concerned with treating all pupils *equally*. In other words, equality of opportunity teaching is concerned with providing experiences that meet each pupil's individual needs, with respect to that pupil's needs in learning in science, and thereby fulfilling the requirements for inclusion. This is such an important area of teaching and learning that it cannot be avoided or ignored. It is a fact that there are differences between pupils, and those differences are to be embraced and used to enhance the curriculum, not regarded as a *problem to overcome*. I will address these areas of equality of opportunity throughout this part of the book, as all may impact on reluctant learners, or be a cause for learners to develop reluctance towards engaging in science; but first I list a number of strategies that can be implemented straight away to ensure you are making your science curriculum accessible and relevant to all your pupils.

- Ensure that you have high expectations for all pupils and convey these to the pupils. Having high expectations does not mean having the same expectation for all pupils; it merely means that you expect all the pupils to succeed in the tasks you provide for them.
- High expectations can be communicated verbally and non-verbally, so do be aware of your own body language.
- Provide tasks that are differentiated to meet all needs – tasks that stretch the learning of all pupils, dependent on their ability, not their attitude towards science. Doing so is important to ensure that reluctant learners are not under-achieving as a result of being given inappropriate work, which will lead to further disengagement.
- Provide learning materials that appeal to all.
- Use your knowledge about the local community to ensure that your teaching is planned with respect to the various cultures and backgrounds that might be present there.
- Challenge your own stereotypical responses (and those of other adults in the classroom). It is easy to think you do not hold stereotypical ideas and do treat everyone fairly and equitably, but think through a recent lesson you have taught

and consider whether any of your responses were inappropriate and based on commonly held stereotypical ideas. Ask another adult who was present in the lesson whether he or she considered any of your responses inappropriate, and, if so, why.

- Consider the groupings of pupils in science: mixed ability, mixed gender, friendship groupings. There is much written about the grouping of pupils, and it is worth reading around the subject in order to make informed judgements. The crucial question is, does the grouping allow for all pupils to be engaged in the lesson and to progress in their learning? In what way does the grouping you have chosen facilitate such progress?

- Develop your own understanding of how mixed-gender and single-gender groups relate to each other. Do the groupings you use enhance the learning or detract from it?

- Establish the *ground rules* for group work – for example, listen to others without interruption, speak in turn, respond to others positively, deal with conflicts and/or disagreements through discussion and reasoned debate, show respect for each member of the group.

- Use praise throughout – for achievements in science and positive attitudes and responses.

Developing independence

As demonstrated throughout the book, learning is a developmental process: taking the ideas learners already hold and building on them until the learners have the knowledge, skills, understandings and attitudes that are commonly held. For learning to take place in this way the learner must be actively involved in the process, must want to learn and want to develop his or her ideas. This learning process is obviously more difficult for the teacher to manage when working with reluctant learners, as their reluctance will severely hinder their progress in learning, and so it is imperative that the teacher devises a curriculum that encourages and stimulates pupils to be actively involved in teaching sessions. The extent to which learners take responsibility for their own learning is dependent on age and maturity. The model shown in

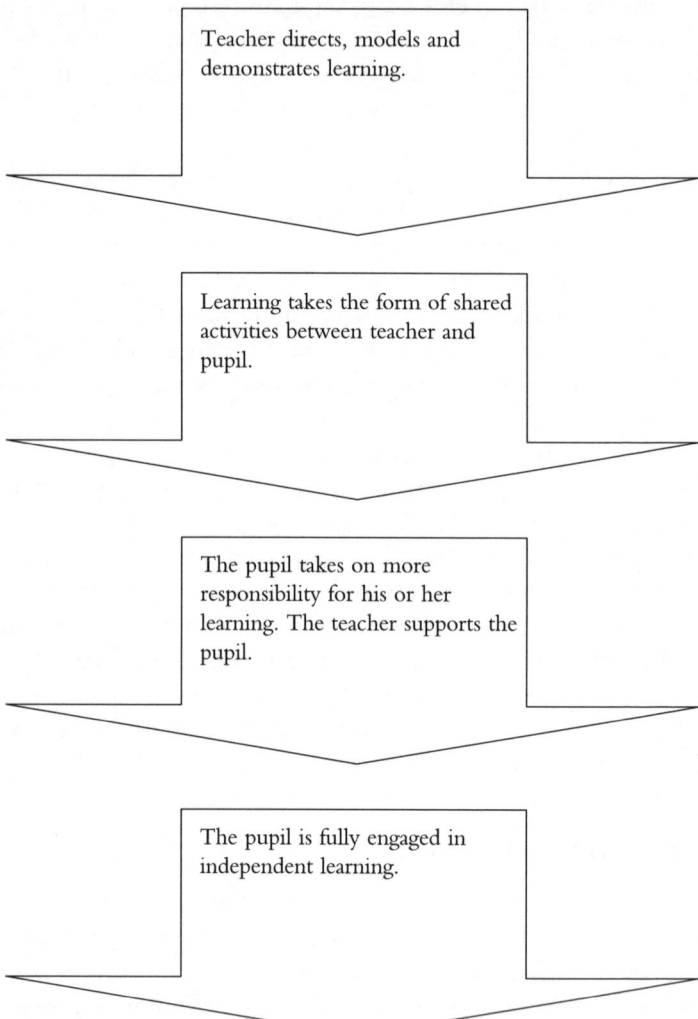

Figure 12.1 Developing independence

Figure 12.1 shows the stages a pupil goes through on the way to becoming an independent learner.

The rate at which pupils move through these stages is dictated by age and maturity, as already noted, but may also be dictated by individual learners' attitudes to learning and to themselves. Reluctant learners therefore may need to spend longer than their peers at one of the stages before independent activities can be expected of them, regardless of their ability in science. This model is therefore helpful for the teacher in identifying the stage of independence in which they are at and in motivating reluctant learners by ensuring their confidence through each of the stages. It can be appreciated that the first three stages rely heavily on a relationship between the adult and pupil and, for pupils who need the support and attention of adults for them to fully engage in the curriculum, the move to independent work may not be what they want as they do not want to lose the support of the adult attention. Although their learning needs point towards movement to the fourth stage, their personal needs may warrant further time spent at the lower stages. It is important for teachers to recognize this in their reluctant learners and to ensure that their learning needs are met by continuing to provide the support and attention such pupils require, while allowing them to progress to the independent stage of learning.

Learning and learning styles

Much is written about the theories of learning and, currently, about preferred learning styles and the effect that preferred learning style has on a learner, in terms of both the learner's engagement with the curriculum and his or her behaviour. Thus, learning styles are a useful starting point for the consideration of the appropriateness of curriculum content and delivery for all learners. This consideration of learning styles is important for the teacher to ensure the motivation and concentration of all pupils. Indeed, good teachers may ask children about their preferred ways of learning.

Learning styles are recognized as the way in which learners take in knowledge, by recognizing it, organizing it, retaining and recalling it. It is accepted that there are four predominant learning styles – visual, auditory, kinaesthetic and tactile.

- *Visual learners* take in information that can be *seen* and so respond to books, displays, words on the board, lists, etc. They recall information by visualizing how it was presented to them.
- *Auditory learners* take in information that is *heard* and so

respond to verbal instructions and make sense of learning
through discussions and general discourse.
- *Kinaesthetic learners* take in information by *movement* and so
learn best when they are actively involved in a task.
- *Tactile learners* take in information through touching, and so
need first-hand experiences when building up learning.

Responding to learning styles involves varying subject content
and presentation styles to match learning styles, as pupils learn
more readily if the teaching methods used match their learning
style. However, a class of pupils is most likely to have groups of
pupils who use each of the learning styles described above, and so
what is needed is for the teacher to use a range of teaching
methods consistently, to ensure that each style is catered for over a
period of time. What is also important is to recognize the
preferred learning styles of individual pupils so that, where
individual reinforcement is needed, the style of reinforcement can
be matched to the individual's learning style. The strategies the
teacher may use to ensure that he or she caters for all the learning
styles include using:

- wall displays, labels, posters, information cards, books, notes
and instructions on the board – to cater for visual learners;
- audio tapes, video tapes, songs, raps, rhymes, paired and
group work and oral instruction – to cater for auditory
learners;
- board games, drama, role play and computer simulations –
to cater for kinaesthetic learners;
- table-top displays, activities that involve handling objects
and observing, investigation and card games – to cater for
tactile learners.

By considering the needs of individual learning styles in this way,
the teacher will be improving learning for all learners and may
reverse the effects of an inappropriate match of teaching style to
learning style. This mismatch of styles may be a cause of
disengagement with the curriculum for some learners, and so
the recognition of the needs of different learning styles may lead to
greater motivation and engagement with the science curriculum.
The teaching of electricity to Key Stage 2 pupils can clearly

illustrate how all learning styles can be catered for while ensuring that the activities are relevant and exciting. To present pupils with a set of electrical components to put together and show them how to light a bulb and how a switch may be used to turn the circuit on and off will fulfil the National Curriculum requirements for the key stage, but will not particularly inspire the pupils. Asking the pupils to make a robot whose eyes flash as it moves is much more inspirational and requires the same depth of knowledge as the first activity. Incidentally, this was one of the first activities I carried out at university during my training and has remained a firm favourite ever since. The activity can be made appropriate to all learning styles.

- The instructions for the activity are recorded on the board and wall displays, labels around the classroom, posters, information cards and books are provided that contain relevant information about the task for the pupil. These are aids for the visual learners in the class who take in information that can be *seen* and recall it by the visualization of how it was presented to them.
- The instructions are also given orally, thereby catering for the auditory learners, who take in information that is *heard*. As with almost all my activities, the activity is carried out in pairs or groups, providing the opportunities for discussion and general discourse that the auditory learners need in order to make sense of their learning.
- The needs of the kinaesthetic learners are met by the use of the context of a three-dimensional object. Kinaesthetic learners learn best when they are actively involved in a task, and so the application of the knowledge of electrical circuits within a moving object is most appropriate.
- Being able to handle the equipment is very important for tactile learners, who take in information through touching and working with objects.

Raising self-esteem

Self-esteem is a crucial issue to consider regarding more reluctant learners but is a very complex issue to address. Pupils develop low self-esteem for a variety of reasons, from their own view of themselves to accepting the views of others, views that may be incorrect and/or based on stereotypes. With respect to the science curriculum, such stereotyping may encourage able pupils to become disengaged from the curriculum, thereby underperforming in order not to attract attention to themselves. Self-esteem and self-image are what dictate a pupil's attitudes and expectations for him- or herself: positive self-attitudes and expectations enable the pupil to meet his or her potential, whereas negative self-attitudes and expectations often become barriers to learning. Ultimately, such negative attitudes and low expectations may result in severe underachievement throughout school, leading to low job aspirations and poor life choices. It can be appreciated just how crucial it is that the teacher uses the curriculum to foster high self-esteem, positive self-attitudes and appropriate expectations. The teacher needs to develop a pupil's self-confidence by ensuring that the science work on offer is structured to promote success and that it is relevant and accessible to all pupils. It is such relevance and accessibility that have been the main themes throughout the book, and those themes continue through this section. An appropriate science curriculum will raise pupils' self-confidence through developing:

- *success* – through a curriculum that values effort and thinking about the process of science;
- *respect* – through valuing each pupil's contribution and acceptance of differences of opinion and interpretation;
- *enthusiasm* – for a science curriculum that is relevant and interesting;
- *creativity* – valuing originality of thought;
- *curiosity* – the eagerness to carry out meaningful investigations;
- *the skills of problem solving* – the ability to consider options, to reason, to make suggestions, to plan and carry out investigations;
- *interest* – in their own and others' explanations of concepts and phenomena;
- *open-mindedness and critical thinking* – to explore the interpretations of scientific evidence.

Celebrating diversity

Both the Race Relations Act 1976 and the Sex Discrimination Act 1975 require schools to promote equal opportunities and positive relations between staff, pupils and parents. There is a legal requirement to work actively towards the elimination of all incidences of discrimination, whether direct or indirect, based on race, colour, ethnic and national origins or gender. It can be appreciated that this is an ongoing commitment for the teacher, that opportunities to explore diversity must be identified and planned for, and that opportunities that arise spontaneously must be dealt with sensitively and meaningfully. In considering such opportunities, the teacher must be mindful of the distinction between teaching *about* equal opportunities and teaching *through* equal opportunities, and must exploit the context that science provides for investigating these two related strands of diversity.

Teaching *about* equal opportunities involves challenging the beliefs of some members of society about other members of society. Stories of scientists, particularly from the past, are an excellent vehicle for exploring discrimination – the reasons for it and the effects of it – and are interesting to discuss with regard to the time the scientist lived and the present day. The story of Maria Mitchell, an American astronomer, is a particularly good story to share with pupils of all ages and can be used to explore attitudes towards the education of females.

Maria, born in 1818, shared her father's interest in astronomy and wanted to study the subject at university. Unfortunately, at the time very few universities were open to females, and so Maria took a job as a librarian. Through her work Maria educated herself, using the books in the library and working alongside her father. In 1847 she was credited with discovering a comet not seen by others. Through this finding she began to travel to talk about her work and her discoveries, and eventually was appointed a professor of astronomy at the Vasser College for Women. Maria continued her own studies in astronomy and became the first scientist to photograph the surface of the sun. Maria died in 1889 after many years of encouraging other women to enter higher education.

Maria's story is not unique for the time; indeed, many women had to overcome such prejudice and unfairness because of their gender. Pupils can use this story to role-play her feelings and those of others of the time: her father, friends, opponents to women in education and Matthew Vasser (the founder of the Vasser College for Women, who asked Maria to become a professor of astronomy). The story can be used to consider the differences in attitude then and now, and what influenced those attitudes for different people.

In contrast, teaching *through* equal opportunities involves ensuring that the curriculum is relevant and accessible for all, as discussed throughout Part Five of the book.

Cultural factors

It is worth noting that cultural factors may affect a pupil's reactions to learning experiences in the classroom. For example, in the primary school a small child who has been brought up not to touch objects without specific permission to do so may not readily involve him- or herself with interactive displays or hands-on activities until encouraged to, and may then need additional support to access the learning involved. Older pupils whose background is one of acceptance of the views of elders without question may not be fully able to engage in discussions or may be reluctant to seek clarification from adults about their work. Although it is important to avoid holding stereotypical ideas about pupils, as discussed elsewhere in this part of the book, it is essential that the teacher is aware that such behaviours exist and may account for pupils' apparent disengagement with the curriculum. Some other issues to consider when planning the science curriculum include the list below.

- Science may be valued in different ways in different cultures and societies, which may influence the pupils' perceptions of the science curriculum being offered.
- The application of science to everyday life must be thought of in terms of the socio-cultural background of the pupils being taught.
- Pupils' prior experiences of science, which should be the basis of science learning, may vary widely, owing to socio-cultural differences.

- It is necessary to avoid ethnic, cultural or gender bias in the contexts of science work and to ensure that the contexts are relevant to all the pupils.
- The language of science is complex; extra support may be needed for pupils who experience language difficulties or who have English as an additional language.

13 Special educational needs

It is a well-used statistic that at any one time 20 per cent of pupils have special educational needs, including special educational needs with regard to the science curriculum. The needs of these children vary widely and include physical disabilities (although not all pupils with physical difficulties will present with special educational needs; some will simply learn alongside their peers using the aids they normally use as part of their daily life, such as a wheelchair or hearing aid), learning difficulties and emotional and behavioural difficulties. In addition, there are children who may be identified as very able, gifted or talented. What is vital is the need to view all pupils, including those with special educational needs, as individuals and to avoid the stereotyping attached to the names of specific conditions or focusing on one aspect of a pupil's needs at the expense of others. Indeed, some pupils experience multiple special educational needs, and to address only one of them would be almost impossible. Reluctant learners may themselves have special educational needs, and so this consideration of the needs of pupils with special educational needs is warranted. It is beyond the scope of this book to provide an in-depth look at each of the different kinds of special needs, and so what I will be presenting are strategies for ensuring a relevant curriculum for all, from the least able pupils to the gifted pupils. What is important to consider is how the science curriculum can be adapted and delivered appropriately to support the scientific learning of all pupils, including those with special educational needs and the reluctant learners, and to ensure that the work is appropriately differentiated for all.

Differentiation

Differentiation is simply the term used to describe how the needs of individual pupils are met within the curriculum on offer, and yet it is a process that many teachers seem to struggle with. It is important for pupils of all ages, abilities and attitudes that the science curriculum provides activities at an appropriate level, in order to ensure full participation in a lesson, thereby leading to effective learning for all pupils. It is this that ensures that the work provides the appropriate challenge for all learners. The process of differentiation begins with knowing the level of ability of each pupil and the next stage needed in their learning, and moves on to the identification of an appropriate learning pathway, one that is supportive, relevant and developmental. Differentiation is therefore an integral part of target setting, as has already been noted in Part Four of the book and will be looked at more fully in Part Seven. The pathway that is indicated through the target-setting cycle will require a consideration of:

- the content of the learning to be delivered;
- the context in which the learning will be set;
- the teaching and learning strategies to be used;
- the support systems that will be put in place;
- the appropriate resources to be provided and used;
- the range of recording methods to be used;
- the assessment methods to be used to assess the learning that has taken place.

Following these considerations, the style of differentiation can then be identified. There are four main styles of differentiation that the teacher may plan to use: differentiation through the input to the activity given by the teacher, through pupil outcome, through the provision of different tasks or by the support of adults or peers.

- *Differentiation by input* is where the teacher adjusts the language he or she uses or the amount of information and instruction he or she supplies depending on the needs and abilities of the pupils. Differentiation by input ensures that less able or less articulate learners are able to access an activity but are not expected to share the same skills in spoken

English as their peers. It is also appropriate for the more able or more articulate, for whom further information can be given or more advanced scientific language introduced.

- *Differentiation by outcome* is probably the most common form of differentiation, whereby the same language and instructions are used with all pupils, who then access the learning by interpreting the task at their own level – for example, recording their ideas about the most suitable habitat for a given animal. The less able will produce a short list or simple features of the habitat, whereas the more able pupils will provide a more extensive and more detailed list of requirements.

- *Differentiation by task* is more complex for the teacher to manage, as it means that all pupils experience the same learning objective but experience it through different tasks that are matched to their ability. Differentiation by task requires the teacher to provide a variety of tasks that are based on one learning objective. For example, when comparing the properties of different materials the less able will be given a different set of materials from those given to the more able and will be given different properties to investigate and possibly a different context for the comparison.

- *Differentiation by support* is much easier to manage, as it merely means the amount and quality of adult or peer support. This additional support is used to ensure that progress is made throughout the lesson and so may involve providing help in carrying out the task, in recording the outcomes of the task and/or in developing understanding of the task.

In addition to these styles of differentiation, pupils with specific special educational needs may need access to more specialist equipment and/or approaches to the curriculum. It is therefore essential that the teacher develop his or her knowledge of the range of special educational needs that pupils may present, and it is essential to involve the school's Special Educational Needs Coordinator's (SENCO) consideration of an appropriate curriculum. The aim of this chapter is to provide an insight into the strategies that may be used with pupils who need extra support in accessing the curriculum, or may need the provision of a more appropriate curriculum, rather than to provide an extensive round-up of commonly occurring special educational needs and how the curriculum can be adapted to each of these needs. Consulting the school's SENCO about specific children and their needs will ensure that relevant, up-to-date advice can be sought, together with the referral to external specialists if warranted.

Helping the least able

Helping the least able requires the teacher to be sympathetic to the pupils' needs and to look for ways to engage them in a relevant curriculum. It can be seen that viewed in these terms, the needs of these pupils are the same as the needs of pupils in general. What is required is a curriculum that, through greater differentiation, is accessible to the pupil and gives the pupil every opportunity to succeed. Some strategies used to allow the less able pupil to access the curriculum, in addition to the other ideas presented in the book, include:

- the use of simplified resources – for example, using texts that the pupil is able to read and understand at his or her level, using resources that convey instructions in a visual format;
- avoiding the use of overly long introductions to activities and/or concepts;
- the use of ICT – for example, instructions given by audio tape;
- using computer simulations to demonstrate ideas;
- using drama, role-play and play to explore themes;
- the use of a series of short activities to deliver the learning objective, rather than one extended activity;
- the use of reinforcement and repetition throughout the activity;
- the relating of work to similar work already completed;
- the use of practical, hands-on activities whenever possible;
- the use of structured methods for written recording (see 'Writing frames', p. 157);

- the use of adult support to scaffold the learning throughout the activity.

The early identification of pupils who require greater support to access the curriculum is crucial, as the failure to recognize the need and to cater for the learning needs of the pupil may result in low self-esteem, frustration, anger and/or cycles of underachievement and alienation. Ultimately, these negative emotions will result in disengagement from the curriculum, with the learner becoming one of our reluctant learners. However, some pupils, particularly pupils with low ability in English, go to great lengths to hide their difficulties, in order not to draw attention to themselves, and so this early identification may be hindered somewhat. It is therefore imperative that all adults involved in a pupil's education are listened to – parents, support staff, outside agencies and the teacher – in order to identify the needs of the less able. The pupil's peers may also contribute to this identification by expressing concerns about the pupil's involvement in group tasks and/or his or her behaviour. One particular strategy that pupils who are experiencing difficulties in their learning, but wish to cover up this difficulty, use is to present a range of behaviour problems. These may include avoidance strategies for engaging in the curriculum and disrupting the learning of others. Here is a fuller list of indicators that the low-ability pupil may exhibit:

- a lack of interest in the curriculum or in school life in general;
- a lack of awareness within a lesson;
- little evidence of, or a reluctance to share, previous experiences in science;
- a lack of interests – in or out of school;
- a reluctance or inability to follow instructions;
- limited speaking and listening skills – including the range of vocabulary used;
- a reluctance to contribute to the lesson – including answering questions, taking part in discussions;
- an apparent lack of concentration and a tendency to be easily distracted;
- significant off-task behaviour: engagement in chatting to peers, involvement in other (often unplanned) activities,

work avoidance strategies;
- attention-seeking behaviour;
- a significant preference for practical activities;
- a lack of interest in instruction cards, books and reading for information;
- an over-reliance on adult support or, conversely, a disregard for adult support;
- a reluctance to complete a task appropriately – by working slowly, or rushing the task, or by pretending to have finished the task in advance of other pupils;
- poor organizational skills, including losing personal property;
- disrupting the learning of others, through inappropriate behaviour or overt strategies for preventing peers from working.

Gifted pupils

A gifted pupil is one who has an ability that is far greater than that of his or her peers. Gifted pupils therefore are not merely bright, but exceptionally so, and yet they may not be easily identified as such. Some of the most reluctant of learners are actually gifted pupils who are disengaged from the curriculum because of boredom and lack of challenge. They may even wish to mask their giftedness so as not to draw attention to themselves. In these instances it is imperative that the culture of the classroom is one that values all abilities and where differentiation is understood not only by the adults but also by the pupils. Gifted pupils may exhibit their giftedness by an overt thirst for knowledge and an ability to recall a broad range of knowledge, often beyond their years. They may be independent workers who do not relate well with their peers during group work, or who take the lead in all group tasks. Once again it is how we respond to gifted pupils as learners that is important, to ensure that the curriculum meets their needs.

One strategy to use would be to offer them science study in greater depth and at a faster pace than is offered to their peers, although this may not meet the needs of reluctant learners who are also gifted. They may first need to become comfortable with their own ability before demonstrating it to their peers. In such a case it may be more appropriate to provide tasks that are open ended and involve *finding out* from a wide range of sources, with additional time built in for the science to be studied at a deeper level. As the pupil becomes more comfortable with his or needs, and begins to engage more fully in an appropriate science curriculum, the following strategies can be introduced:

- the use of more challenging scientific vocabulary by the teacher and expected from the pupil;
- the opportunity to extend tasks beyond the point at which their peers end the task – for example, to extend the work to encompass the requirements of the next key stage of the National Curriculum;
- the opportunity to solve more demanding problems;
- the opportunity to direct their own study, such as by identifying, with the teacher, appropriate areas and/or contexts to study and then carrying out independent investigations and research into the area;
- using and applying scientific ideas and skills in a range of (different) contexts; again these may be indicated by the requirements of the next key stage in the National Curriculum;
- the opportunity to work with gifted students and/or adults beyond the school – via e-mail, letters, visits to other institutions.

It must be remembered that you are catering for the gifted pupil's needs, that your responsibility is to provide suitable challenge for the pupil with the requirement to advance their learning at an appropriate pace for them. It is not merely a case of occupying an active mind! The worst strategy to use with the gifted pupil who is also a reluctant learner is to ask the pupil to carry out an in–depth study of his or her own choice. Although this may appear to be the best strategy, as it allows for the pupil's own interests to be used, and allows the learner to work at a pace that suits him or her *and* to study the topic in depth, it does not inspire the gifted child who has been given this instruction many times before. It is the role of the teacher therefore to identify activities that are most suited to the learner, a strategy that provides opportunities for the pupil to be involved in directing his or her own learning while also ensuring that meaningful learning is taking place.

Providing additional support

It is important to recognize that many pupils require support at some point in the course of their learning; the support to be considered here is that which is needed in addition to the normal support given through the course of your teaching. The identification of the need for such support will most likely arise through assessments you have made, as noted in Chapter 10, although it is accepted that reluctant learners may need greater support in terms of accessing the curriculum. This support may take many forms, from additional information regarding a task to a detailed explanation of the outcome of the task, from interesting pupils in the task to maintaining their interest through to the end of the task. For reluctant learners this additional support may be crucial for their engagement and success in the science curriculum.

I am concentrating on three specific forms of additional support for learning: adult support, peer support and support for writing. Adult support above all can be extremely motivating for a pupil, as is noted throughout the book, but the support must be focused on ensuring access to the curriculum rather than on simplifying the tasks unnecessarily. Indeed, adult expectations, and behaviour, have a powerful impact upon pupil aspirations, achievement and self-esteem, and so must be exploited. There are some pupils, not all of whom are reluctant learners, who prefer not to seek adult help and guidance, and so the use of peer support can aid these learners in their learning and, in turn, promote learning for the peer giving support, as is outlined later in the chapter. Support in the form of writing frames is not technically additional support, as the use of frames across the curriculum is an everyday occurrence, and has already been touched on in Chapter 8. However, I believe that they may be classed as additional support if they are used to support learning where to not use them would put the learner at a disadvantage in his or her learning.

Adult support

The use and quality of adult support can be crucial to the access of the curriculum by the reluctant learner. The adult providing the additional support must:

- demonstrate positive attitudes between adult and pupil;
- establish a learning culture in which the ethos is supportive of all pupils;
- hold high expectations of all pupils;
- exploit positive adult–pupil interactions;
- share learning experiences with the pupils;
- engender belief in the pupils;
- use verbal and non-verbal communication to demonstrate his or her understanding of the pupils' needs;
- recognize the pupils' personal and cultural experiences and backgrounds;
- recognize the individual needs of the pupils.

The support must, as already stated, ensure that pupils access the curriculum at an appropriate level. The support is needed to help pupils engage with the task, with maintaining their engagement and motivation and in completing the task. The adult support must not simplify the task below the level that is appropriate to a particular learner, as this will not meet the learner's needs and may lead to further disengagement from science and science study – and the adult must certainly not complete the task for the pupil! It is the teacher's responsibility to ensure that the adult providing the additional support knows what is expected of him or her. This expectation of adults within the curriculum will be considered further in Parts Six and Seven of the book.

Peer support

To ignore the positive benefits of peer support would be to remove an essential strategy in the teaching of science. Peer support is vital for learners who are reluctant to engage with adults and, as science is accepted as a social subject, ensures that learners are able to develop their ideas through discussion. Peer support takes many forms, from offering increased confidence for pupils lacking in the confidence necessary for engaging in the curriculum, to scaffolding the learning of one or more members of a group engaged on a particular task. The requisites of peer support are that the pupils:

- are able to relate appropriately to their peers;
- have a degree of open-mindedness so as to be able to accept and discuss the ideas of others;
- are willing to accept that there may be differences of opinion;
- have the skills to deal with differences of opinion;
- need to be confident in their own learning if they are offer support to others;
- recognize the classroom procedures to be followed.

To develop peer support in the science classroom and to build up these requisites necessitate training by the teacher. Pupils need to be taught the social skills necessary for supporting the learning of others and being supported in their own learning, for peer support is a two-way process. By supporting the learning of others, pupils are able to assess their own learning that is taking place and to identify their own future learning needs.

Peer support may take place through group work or through paired working. When promoting support through group work, the teacher must be mindful of the need to ensure that each pupil in the group has a role, thereby reducing the opportunity for a pupil needing support to withdraw from the task, either mentally or physically. Peer support through paired work is much easier to manage, and ensures that both pupils are able to develop a shared understanding through a discussion of the learning experience.

Writing frames

Using a variety of communication and recording techniques, to ensure that pupils experience a range of ways to describe and explain their ideas about science, is a central approach for ensuring that the science curriculum is accessible for all. By providing this variety over a period of time, teachers cater for all learners, all learning needs and all learning styles. However, it must be remembered that in science lessons it is the quality of the science learning that is of paramount importance, not the pupil's ability in the conventions of English, and so the provision of aids for recording science work in writing in the form of writing frames or structures is a valuable strategy for working with reluctant learners. Although there is no requirement to record all science work in writing, pupils do need to develop the skills for this form of writing for two reasons: written recording in science will support the teaching and learning of literacy, as described in Chapter 8, and written recording is demanded in external tests. For these reasons it is therefore essential that the pupil develop the necessary skills, and by providing a model for the pupils to follow, the teacher is supporting the learners in acquiring the skills while also ensuring their success with the immediate task. By extending the opportunities for using such frames, the teacher is providing additional support for learning where it is needed. However, the teacher must be mindful of when it is appropriate to remove this additional support, to prevent pupils' over-reliance on this support strategy.

There are many examples of writing frames to be found in books or on the Internet, and researching them is time well spent by the teacher. Using such frames then aids the teacher in developing his or her own supports and builds confidence in the learner. Two particular types of frames I have used in science are those provided Feasey (1999) and the skeletons for writing poster books by Sue Palmer (www.suepalmer.co.uk). Writing frames may be used:

- to provide an outline for how the text is to be organized;
- to provide the main language to be used;
- to provide a structure related to a specific genre, e.g. a report, a letter, an explanation;
- to record the planning of science work;
- to record the method of science work;
- to record the outcomes of science work.

Writing frames therefore support pupils in their recording by providing a structure that enables pupils to concentrate on the *content* of the information they wish to communicate, rather than on *how to organize* their writing. They ensure that the written outcome is not purely narrative or simply descriptive but is moving towards being analytical and explanatory in nature, by providing a framework containing key words and/or phrases, starters, connectives and sentence modifiers. Using such frames also ensures that children become familiar with the requirements of a particular writing structure. Regular use of a variety of frames provides pupils with a bank of structures to draw on when asked to record work without the use of a frame. Frames can also be used to support pupils in their research of information by organizing the recording of key facts, thus ensuring that they do not copy copious amounts of text from the source or print pages of information from the Internet.

14 Science and behaviour

There are many factors involved in the development of positive behaviour in the classroom. What is important in science is that the classroom environment appears inviting, interesting and stimulating, and encourages the notion that the science work on offer will be exciting and relevant to the pupil. The use of positive discipline and praise is essential. It is important to establish the rules of the classroom, including the rules for safe working practices. The rules must be stated simply but explicitly, with an expectation that they will be adhered to. It is also important to model the behaviours you wish to encourage in the classroom; one of the ways of doing so is to develop your own daily practice and ensure you use it consistently. Some features of good daily practice you may wish to develop are listed below.

- Make a clear, crisp start to each lesson – ensuring that no time is lost and the pace of the lesson is set from the outset.
- Demonstrate your own interest in and enthusiasm for the lesson. If you're not interested, you can hardly expect the pupils to work with enthusiasm.
- Share the lesson's objectives with the pupils, so that they know why they are engaging in an activity and what they are expected to achieve through it. It is here that you establish the relevance of the work you are offering.
- Recap on previous relevant science work – to demonstrate the learning and experiences you are building on.
- Know the direction in which you want the lesson to go, but be open to other ideas and interpretations.
- Demonstrate high expectations of yourself, the pupils and the lesson.

- Offer clear instructions and explanations, and use appropriate, sequenced questions to develop the learning.
- Provide high-quality resources that are relevant and meaningful to the task.
- Maintain the pace of the lesson while ensuring that there is adequate time for the pupils to carry out their investigations.
- Ensure that the learning taking place through the activity is consolidated – by using the end of the lesson to recap and reinforce the intended learning objective.
- Provide high-quality feedback throughout the lesson – feedback on progress, ways of working and responses and indicating areas for improvement.

One category of special educational needs to note is that of pupils experiencing emotional and behavioural difficulties (EBD). As with all categories of SEN, this is a complex one, with no simple *quick-fix* answers! Pupils with EBD may exhibit a wide range of behaviours, from disruption and aggression towards peers to attention seeking and displaying a poor self-image. The behaviour displayed is usually extreme in nature. The causes of these patterns of behaviour are far from simple, and so the management of them may be quite challenging for the teacher. The pupils themselves often do not enjoy the behaviour they display but may or may not be willing partners in its management. What is important when working with such pupils is not to allow the behaviour they display to become the focus of attention within a teaching session, but if the behaviour has to be addressed by the teacher, it is the *behaviour* that is dealt with, not the pupil. The golden rule is that the pupil and his or her learning are paramount within the lesson; the behaviour is addressed only if it impinges on that learning.

Further strategies to be employed in the science lesson, in addition to the good daily practice set out above, when working with pupils who exhibit EBD or with classes that display more overt difficulties in maintaining appropriate behaviours throughout a teaching session, include the following list.

- Structure the lesson tightly; ensure that the whole of the lesson time is used for directed activities.

- Use directed activities to reduce the need for pupils to make choices.
- Use clearly worded, direct statements and instructions.
- Reduce the number of questions asked of individual pupils.
- Use answer boards for pupils to answer questions on. Each pupil then holds up his or her board showing that pupil's response. All pupils are therefore involved in all questioning.
- Keep tasks short, focused and with clear outcomes that are shared with pupils throughout the lesson. The ideas for ten-minute activities presented in Chapter 4 can be used most effectively here.

As behaviours improve, it is important to remove these extra support systems by building up the time spent on longer tasks and on discussions. It is important to use praise throughout – praise for progress made in science and also for progress made in developing appropriate behaviours. Be clear about the behaviours you expect. Share these expectations with the pupils and praise them for moving towards these expectations. As the teacher in charge of the learning, you must develop the insight to identify when disruptive behaviour is building up and then defuse it. One very effective strategy here is to use your sense of humour. Making a whimsical comment can often ease tension in the classroom and redirect attention to the teacher rather than to an unwanted behaviour. Try to identify the triggers for disruptive behaviour and work to avoiding them, possibly by changing groupings of pupils, the layout of the room or the types of activity you use.

This has been a very brief consideration of what can be a vast area to address. Once again, the ideas I have presented are merely starting points for you to consider and to aid you in identifying where behaviour issues impact on the reluctant learner and to aid you in developing the bank of strategies you are able to draw on.

Continuity and progression

There is nothing more disheartening for the teacher than to hear a pupil exclaim, 'We've done this before'. It is also one of the major causes of disengagement with the curriculum, as the pupils, particularly the more able pupils, immediately become bored, and reluctant to be involved in something they not only have done before but also know well. It is also one of the major causes of low-level disruption in the classroom, and so it is therefore imperative for the teacher to know that the experiences he or she is providing are new and exciting, and will lead to the furthering of the pupils' knowledge, skills, understandings and/or attitudes. This is where school planning for continuity and progression is needed.

Continuity and progression are two requisites that are often used as a single term to express the idea that learning experiences must build upon each other. Continuity is actually the need for a connection in the learning, so that each learning experience is not fragmented but can be appreciated as being relevant to other learning, while progression is the moving forward of learning by building on existing skills, knowledge, understandings and attitudes. The teacher must therefore have knowledge of the science work that has been carried out and the levels of achievements of the pupils. Much of this knowledge will have been provided through the assessment information passed on, as described in Chapter 10, and through the record of learning, to be discussed in Chapter 17. Knowledge of the long-term planning for science within the school will also provide information about the science work indicated for each year group. It is important that the long-term plan provides for a coherent and uniform approach to science, delivered through practical, investigative and research tasks, together with the need to build on existing skills, knowledge, understanding, values and attitudes – as suggested by the central theme of this book.

Through addressing the needs of continuity and progression, the teacher will be addressing the need to provide every pupil with the opportunity to succeed in his or her learning and to achieve as high a standard as possible. Addressing continuity and progression ensures that pupils have a developmental curriculum that is flexible in approach yet based on high expectations, while being mindful of individual needs of pupils. It also ensures that the same activity is not presented to pupils year after year!

Part Six

Science outside the Curriculum

15 Celebrating science

I have stated more than once already that the documentation for science provides only a minimum requirement for the science curriculum. I also believe that science is sufficiently motivating for it not to be restricted to the designated curriculum time only – that it lends itself to study outside the curriculum. If science is celebrated beyond the curriculum, the perception of science by adults and pupils alike will become more positive and may be motivational for the reluctant learner. Indeed, the reluctant learner may regard the science curriculum *hard work*, whereas science beyond the curriculum may be considered *fun* and *exciting*. Interesting the reluctant learner through experiences of science beyond the curriculum, and relating them to the curriculum, may encourage him or her to re-engage with the formal curriculum on offer.

There are many ways in which science may be extended beyond the curriculum; the following are my top ten.

1. making science a focus for an assembly;
2. running a science club or science drop-in session for pupils and/or parents;
3. producing a science newsletter for pupils and/or parents;
4. planning a science-themed evening for parents and other adults;
5. planning a science-themed week in school;
6. a visit out of school hours to a science centre;
7. a visiting theatre company putting on a science-themed play;
8. pupils presenting science to governors;
9. in-school competitions;
10. entering science-based competitions out of school.

Science assemblies

There are many themes for assembly that link well to science and keep science a topic for discussion. Many schools have weekly assemblies where work from the curriculum is shown. Science work should definitely feature here, in order to drive home the message that science is fun, is exciting and is worth sharing. For reluctant learners who may struggle with literacy and numeracy, sharing their own or others' successful science work may encourage them to further engage in scientific study.

In addition to sharing work, the stories of scientists may be used to illustrate a religious or moral theme being made. One of my favourite stories for an assembly theme was taken from Feasey (1999) and is the story of a black American scientist who set up a blood bank system in England. It is a very poignant story that illustrates well the prejudiced attitudes that were held at the time of his death (1950) and may well be held by some people today, and the effects of such discriminatory behaviour. I have provided a very short version of the story below; the longer version can be found in Feasey's book *Primary Science and Literacy*.

Charles Drew

Charles Drew, a black American scientist, was born on 3 June 1904, the oldest of five children, and lived in Washington, DC. Although he wanted to be a doctor, his parents couldn't afford to send him to medical school and so he took a job coaching athletes so as to earn enough money to train as a doctor.

In 1928 he attended McGill University Medical School and in 1933 he qualified as a doctor, receiving both the 'Master of Surgery' and 'Doctor of Medicine' qualifications.

It was during his training that Charles became interested in the problem of collecting, storing and keeping blood. He made many advances in this area, and during the Second World War he became involved in setting up a military blood-bank system. He was acknowledged worldwide as an expert in this area and, because of his expertise, was asked to set up a blood-bank system in Britain, the foundation of our present blood transfusion service.

It was in 1950, when Charles was back in the United States, that he himself needed a blood transfusion. He was involved in a serious car crash and needed treatment, including a blood transfusion. However, at this time in the United States there were 'whites only' and 'black' hospitals, with blood from black and white donors also being segregated. Charles was first taken to a 'whites only' hospital but was refused treatment there because of his colour; he was then taken to the nearest 'black' hospital but died on the way. He was aged 46. Ironically, the work he had dedicated his life to could have saved his life, but because of the prejudices of the time this was not to be.

The retelling of this story offers so much to an assembly theme, not least the real-life application of science and the benefit to everyone of studying science, the effects of science and the lives and work of scientists. The stories of many other scientists may also be used in this way. What I find most interesting, and upsetting, about the story of Charles Drew is the fact that he died for the want of what he had made possible for others: a blood transfusion. This raises many issues to discuss about prejudice and how times have changed.

Scientific concepts and theories also make suitable themes for assembly. Another favourite of mine is to compare the Big Bang theory of how the universe was created and the theory of evolution to the Creation story in the Bible. A simple comparison shows that scientists agree with the order of events in the Creation story in the forming of the world, space, plants and animals (including people). The use of other creation stories from other faiths leads to a discussion on beliefs, and the importance of beliefs to religion – and on the fact that scientists may also hold religious beliefs. This theme again this demonstrates to the pupils how scientific theories are relevant to them and can provoke discussions between both scientists and non-scientists.

Science clubs

Science clubs or informal drop-in sessions, for pupils and/or parents, are yet another means of engaging pupils and their parents in science, and for spreading the message that science study can be fun and is relevant to all. However, such clubs are run out of school hours, and so it may be that some reluctant learners will not attend them. Indeed, if they are reluctant to engage in learning during school hours, it may be unrealistic to expect them to engage with out-of-hours teaching! Nevertheless, running a club is an important addition to the school curriculum, and reluctant learners may be enthused by peers talking about the club, by parents attending the club or by the club activities being shared in assembly. For reluctant learners, joining a club may provide the opportunity for scientific study without the pressure to succeed in the classroom. It may also invoke feelings of belonging and that what they are participating in is worthwhile – *and* that their contributions are valued.

There are many considerations and decisions to be made when setting up and running a successful science club.

- Successful clubs do not have to be run by teachers. Following the Workforce Reform guidance, it may be preferable for a member of the support staff or a parent to take the lead in setting up and running the club, with the teacher providing ideas and guidance when and where needed.
- The club is not a formal lesson, and this should be taken into account when planning the activities to be carried out. The activities need not relate to the documentation for science and need not be recorded by the pupils.
- The pupils should be encouraged to participate in the running of the club, by suggesting ideas for club activities, bringing in ideas and snippets from magazines and television programmes, etc.
- The atmosphere should be relaxed, and the pace dictated by the members of the club.
- The adult should take more of a role as a facilitator: providing ideas, resources and information when requested or to guide the pupils if needed.
- Discussion, questioning and reasoning should all be encouraged.
- Pupils of different ages will attend the club, and so the organizer must be mindful of their differing needs and actively work to ensure that the club and its activities are relevant to all its members.
- The club is a social gathering, and so again the organizer

must be mindful of the needs of pupils to work together and discuss their activities in an informal manner.

Running a science club provides the freedom to cover a wide range of activities, and the only constraints are the organizer's creativity and imagination. A valuable source of advice for setting up and running a science club is the website of the British Association for the Advancement of Science (www.the-ba.net). In addition to the ideas on offer, the website also provides links to other relevant websites, including:

- SciZmic – the science discovery clubs network. This site provides ideas, details of events and competitions, but the main function is to put science clubs in contact with each other. (www.scizmic.net)
- SETNET – the Science, Engineering, Technology and Mathematics Network. SETNET is a charity that promotes science, technology, engineering and mathematics (STEM) awareness; the site provides ideas and contacts for visitors into school. (www.setnet.org.uk)
- Science Live – the science presenters' directory. This is an online guide to science presenters and shows, and is designed to help teachers to arrange visits from science presenters. (www.sciencelive.net)

Together these websites will provide you with almost all the information you need for setting up and maintaining a science club. The websites may also be accessed by the pupils in order for them to be fully involved in the club and the activities it offers.

Science newsletters

All schools send out documentation to parents from time to time. The documentation may take various forms, such as brochures, booklets or newsletters. Such documentation is essential for keeping parents informed of school events, and the inclusion of information regarding science in school in the documentation is yet another means of communicating the importance of science to the parents and, in turn, to the pupils. The production of a newsletter that is exclusive to science will further this message about the importance, relevance and excitement of science.

The content of a science newsletter cannot be prescribed, although one prerequisite must be the inclusion of pupils' work, to demonstrate the range of work in science carried out through the formal science curriculum in school. Depending upon the age of the pupils, they should be involved in the publication of the newsletter. The newsletter's prime purpose must be to promote an interest in science, within the curriculum and beyond, to advertise forthcoming science events and to recognize achievements in science. Although, as I say, the contents of a successful newsletter cannot be prescribed, here are my top ten items to include.

1. details of school themed events – already carried out and those yet to be carried out;
2. information about the school's science club or drop-in sessions, with an invitation to join in;
3. invitations to help in science in school;
4. an investigation to try at home;
5. a science competition to complete at home and a date for submission to school;
6. samples of pupils' work – both from the formal curriculum and from the science club;
7. science news items from around the world;
8. an invitation to the next science event to be held in school, together with full details of the event;
9. news of any science competition winners, in school or out of school, and the latest achievements in science of pupils past and present;
10. a request for further items to include in the newsletter.

In order to keep the interest generated by the publication and issuing of a science newsletter going, it is important to decide how often the newsletter can be produced and to ensure that it is produced and issued on a regular basis. It is easy in these busy times to *forget* to work on the newsletter, and yet for pupils, the motivational aspect of working on the newsletter is well worth the effort involved.

Themed events

Themed events are excellent for raising the profile of science for pupils, staff, parents and governors. They allow the school to concentrate on science, the importance of scientific study and the relevance of science to everyday life for an extended period of time. Immersing the school in science thinking means that *all* learners are encouraged to take part and to value the experiences.

Themed evenings for parents and governors are an essential vehicle for enhancing others' perceptions of how science is taught and what pupils learn. It is important for the pupils to be involved, as *the proof of the pudding is in the eating*, and so the pupils are needed to demonstrate their ideas, thoughts and resulting work from the science curriculum. Involving reluctant learners in planning and presenting this type of evening will be motivational for them and again free them from what they perceive to be the demands of the curriculum. Parents of reluctant learners may be enthused by the events, and their child's involvement in them, and pass this enthusiasm on to their child.

Dedicated curriculum weeks or days are motivational for staff and children alike. They are appropriate events for inviting parents to help or to participate in, and may lead to parents having increased confidence in helping their child, both in school and at home. Each year the National Science Week takes place in March; this is a festival promoted by the British Association for the Advancement of Science (BA) and is a good opportunity for schools to plan their own science week or day. The BA website (www.the-ba.net) can provide ideas for a focus for the week or day, together with further ideas for both visits out of school and visitors into school.

The dedicated days are superb for ensuring that science has a high profile across the school and that pupils of all ages are engaged in related study in science. At my school we have had many themes for our dedicated days including a whole-school investigation using Play-Doh, 'Weather Watch' (in which each class recorded the weather each day in a style of their choosing), the life and work of a scientist or inventor, a science trail around the school grounds – devised by Year 6 pupils and then used by other pupils.

Other science-themed events that are particularly motivational for the reluctant learner include:

- a visit out of school hours to a science centre – for pupils, parents, staff and governors;
- a visiting theatre company providing a science-based play for all pupils to enjoy;
- a presentation of science to governors – pupils to keep the governors informed about the science curriculum in practice;
- pupils scripting and performing their own science-based play or show;
- writing and presenting an evening of science-inspired poetry and stories;
- in-school competitions – for example, a poetry-writing competition based on a science concept, or a question of the week to research and then present to an audience;
- a school science newspaper or magazine written and published by pupils. This could include stories, competitions, rhymes, etc. and be based on the adult newsletter version;
- entering a competition out of school – within the local education authority (LEA) or run by an outside agency such as the BA.

All the ideas presented in this chapter are aimed at ensuring that the importance and relevance of science study are communicated to both pupils and adults, and are intended to inspire and engage pupils and adults so that they become involved in science in school and beyond. It is vital that today's pupils, and adults, develop an appreciation and an understanding of scientific issues and can both discuss and reason about the issues in a confident and informed way. By extending the study of science in the ways suggested, we are promoting this ability to appreciate and understand a range of scientific issues and are encouraging pupils to develop the skills needed to discuss and reason about the issues.

16 Science and adults

Throughout the book I have talked about the importance of other adults in the delivery of the formal science curriculum and other studies in science both beyond the curriculum and beyond the school day. It is therefore important that the teacher becomes comfortable with working with a range of adults, including:

- support staff;
- parents;
- governors;
- LEA representatives;
- visitors;
- specialist teachers;
- outside agencies;
- any other adults working in the school.

Developing positive working relationships with all these groups of adults is important, as each group can both impact on the science curriculum and extend science study beyond the confines of the curriculum.

Working with parents

Developing a good relationship with parents is an essential for:

- informing the parents as to what constitutes the science curriculum;
- ensuring that the parents have an understanding of the skills, concepts and understandings their child will be developing in school;
- establishing a relevant curriculum for the pupil;
- ensuring that the parents are confident in supporting their child in science;

- encouraging the parents to exhibit positive attitudes towards science, both in school and beyond;
- encouraging parents to carry out scientific activities with their child at home to lend support;
- developing motivation in the child;
- encouraging parents who happen to possess particular scientific knowledge, understanding and/or skills themselves to support the teacher with other pupils in school.

Working with parents, and forming appropriate relationships, is a skill in itself, and is an important skill to acquire, as a positive, supportive relationship between teacher and parent is a powerful aid to motivating reluctant learners. However, as noted at the beginning of the book, many adults have a negative way of thinking towards science, particularly science studied in school; if a pupil's parents hold such negative views and pass these on to their child, then it can be more easily understood why we have reluctant learners in school. On the other hand, if by working with the parents we can develop in them more positive attitudes, in turn they may be able to motivate and enthuse their child to engage in the science offered in school. In addition to the ideas presented here for working with parents, the ideas contained in Chapter 15 will certainly aid in informing parents of what modern school science is all about.

Working with parents requires a range of interpersonal skills that are needed to relate to adults in a non-threatening manner. The aim is to ensure that parents are at ease when visiting school and discussing the work their child is carrying out, and are knowledgeable about the details of the curriculum. For some parents this may be the norm; for others it will be quite an unnerving experience, particularly if their own school days were less than successful. Some tips I have acquired for working with parents include the following:

- Smile! Show that you are pleased to see the parent and are willing to discuss curriculum issues.
- Invite parents into school to work alongside their child in the classroom and beyond.
- Invite parents to themed events.
- Seek to understand parental points of view.

- Know the child!
- Be able to discuss the curriculum with reference to the individual child.
- Develop an understanding of how parents are able to help their child at home – that is, techniques parents may use, or games they can play, to consolidate work taught in school.
- Develop strategies for teaching parents; a parent may need to be taught the science being studied before he or she is able to support the child.
- Show appreciation of the fact that school is building on learning begun by the child's parents and that you are encouraging parents to continue as active partners in their child's ongoing learning
- Assure the parents that they and the pupils are able to carry out quality scientific enquiry, involving observation and discussion, rather than their having to find the *right* answer or the correct theory.

Encouraging parental interest in science may require a range of strategies. The teacher may know some parents well and may be able to approach them directly yet informally. Alternatively, the teacher may need to encourage a reluctant parent to engage in the science curriculum him- or herself! This may take time, but enthusing the parent is particularly important in the case of a reluctant learner, as stated many times already, and so it is vital that the teacher demonstrate enthusiasm and make science a focus in the classroom. This is achieved by:

- displaying pupils' work in science in and around the classroom, preferably with work in other subjects to demonstrate the relevance of science to everyday life and to the whole curriculum;
- displaying short-term and medium-term planning in the classroom, to inform parents of what their child is studying and how it relates to their studies across the curriculum;
- inviting parental involvement in science by placing an invitational poster on the wall;
- providing homework in science, presented in an interesting format;

- publishing a booklet or pamphlet on how parents may support their child's learning in science at home;
- arranging a weekly science club or drop-in session for parents and pupils.

Working with governors and local education authority representatives

The skills needed for working with parents and forming suitable relationships with them are also indicated for the teacher to work with and relate to the school's governors and to LEA representatives. The governing body is responsible for the establishment of school policies and practices and so it is important that governors too are knowledgeable about what constitutes an effective, innovative, relevant and exciting science curriculum; LEA representatives are an excellent support for schools and an excellent resource for knowledge about current trends in education. Many of the ideas associated with working with parents are therefore more than fitting for working with the governors of the school and with LEA representatives.

Working with other adults

A consideration of working with adults in science would be incomplete if it did not cover working with adults other than teachers in the school – that is, the support staff, visitors, members of outside agencies and volunteers, together with specialist teachers in the school. In order to motivate reluctant learners, *all* adults working with such pupils must interest and engage them in the work on offer. The most effective way of stimulating interest is to lead by example, and so the teacher may also be able to enthuse and motivate all other adults involved in a science lesson. It is therefore vital for the teacher to form good working relationships with these adults and to ascertain their views and attitudes towards science: although it must be accepted that many adults have negative attitudes towards science, it must also be accepted that many other adults have positive attitudes towards it! The other adults involved in the lesson may therefore be enthusiastic about science themselves, and may then be able to enthuse the pupils they are supporting in various ways, indeed in ways that the teacher may also benefit and learn from. Again, many of the ideas for working with parents presented earlier in this chapter are also applicable to working with the range of other adults in school. In addition to these ideas, the teacher must make time to talk through scientific activities with the supporting adults, in order to ensure that they are confident in the science they are involved in and are able to support the pupils in engaging with the scientific study.

Visitors to school are a particular group of adults who warrant specific mention. A well-prepared, knowledgeable visitor can bring science truly alive for even the most reluctant of learners, although it must be reiterated that *all* learners are different and so there is no one sure-fire winner for engaging the reluctant learner, as needs vary. Therefore, the use of visitors within science is simply one of many strategies to use to ensure that science is accessible by all pupils. However, the use of visitors in science – people who can talk about and demonstrate their experiences of science – can be very stimulating for a range of pupils. Again, working with visitors is a skill for the teacher to attain and is a skill well worth working on, for both the teacher and the pupils.

Perhaps the main consideration for the teacher is to be mindful that the visitor may be very knowledgeable, enthusiastic and motivational, but he or she is not the teacher in charge of the class! You must remain in charge and ensure that the occasion of having an expert in to share his or her experiences is a positive one. You must be able to make the visitor comfortable and relaxed. Allow the visitor to direct the session while ensuring both the good behaviour and the interest of the pupils. For the visit to be a positive experience for all, and for the pupils to gain the maximum educational benefit from the visitor, it is essential that both the pupils and the visitor are prepared for the meeting. Such preparation includes both being briefed about the topic or concept area to be covered. The pupils need to have prepared their own questions for the visitor, and the visitor needs to have taken the time to prepare notes and other sources of information to aid him or her at the meeting. This caveat may sound as if the preparation needed makes the event more trouble than it's worth! That is certainly not the case.

Suggested visitors include:

- people whose daily work is science related, for example a chemist;
- people whom science aids in their everyday life, such as a gardener;
- museum or science centre staff;
- adults willing to take on the role of a famous scientist such as Charles Darwin.

In addition to the preparations for the visitor in school detailed above, the visitor will also need an outline of the work the pupils have already carried out regarding the science theme, the background to the topic and an insight into the interests and ability level of the pupils. The pupils will also need to be informed that a visitor is to join the class and need to know who the visitor is and what sort of information he or she will be able to provide.

This amount of preparation will ensure that the visitor contributes to the science curriculum and furthers the pupils' work and interest in the science curriculum.

Part Seven
Final Thoughts

17 Keeping science going

It is obviously most important to maintain a pupil's interest in science, particularly for the reluctant learner who you may have only recently engaged in science and science study, and so you may now need to consider how you are going to ensure that your pupils continue to enjoy interesting and exciting yet relevant science activities. I do hope that the ideas I have presented throughout the book have whetted your own appetite for devising such activities and you are sufficiently inspired to search the Internet and/or library shelves for more ideas. (Part Eight of the book does make suggestions for where you may start to look for more ideas.) My final thoughts for you are therefore about how you can keep science going by building on the ideas I have already presented. First I will look at time issues within science teaching and how you may use the time available. Next I will explain the need to keep up-to-date records of your teaching and learning in science, and thus the attainment of all your pupils. I will then return to the subject of target setting, which will draw together many of the strands of the book, from using assessments and the documentation for science to providing a relevant science curriculum for all learners through the accurate identification of appropriate activities. I will end this part of the book with a further look, in Chapter 18, at working with others, and how this can keep science going in your classroom.

Time issues

You need to decide whether your science delivery will consist of short but intensive bursts of science teaching, or whether a more continuous approach to your science teaching would be preferable. Within secondary schools, science is timetabled regularly each week, and often sessions are allocated to a particular strand of the science curriculum – that is, to physics, chemistry and biology – and yet this consideration may also help you to decide how long you will focus on one particular topic, concept or skill. Within the primary school and nurseries there is often a greater timetable freedom, although here too there may be weekly timetabled slots for science. It is obviously important that you work within the school's planning for science delivery, but if there is flexibility available, then do consider how and when you are going to deliver the science curriculum.

The benefits of teaching science intensively in the primary school for a short period of time are that motivation for the pupil is maintained, learning is built upon rapidly, ideas can be studied in depth and a seemingly large amount of science can be covered in quite a short space of time. The downside is that, following this intense burst, science may not be covered in any depth for some time, to allow for other curriculum subjects to be covered. This may result in the learning being *lost*, as it is not consolidated, and interest in science study may wane.

The benefit of teaching science continuously – that is, teaching a topic through weekly activities, using dedicated weekly slots in the timetable – is that science knowledge, skills, understandings and attitudes are developed systematically and gradually. The time for practice and consolidation is built in, with the added benefit that the learning is not lost through being forgotten in the times between the study of science, as it is with intensive teaching. The downside is that the spreading of the science work over a few weeks may reduce its impact on the pupil and lead to loss of interest and demotivation for science study, particularly in the case of reluctant learners who find it both difficult to remember the science work carried out the previous week and difficult to see the links between the activities presented. Also, the pupils' ideas may not always be followed through, because of time constraints, which again can be demotivating for them, particularly the more reluctant learners.

It can be appreciated that both these approaches to science – short intensive bursts and the weekly timetabled slots – can provide worthwhile study and benefits for all learners. Probably the best approach therefore would be a combination of the two approaches, if possible. This can be achieved by deciding:

- which parts of the science curriculum are best delivered continuously – for example, the parts that need most consolidation and practice;
- which parts of the science curriculum are best taught intensively for short, concentrated bursts of time;
- which parts of the science curriculum can be addressed through short ten-minute activities as and when the slots arise, as described in Chapter 4.

Once you have identified these parts of the curriculum, the areas to be taught continuously can be delivered through the planned weekly sessions, and the intensive short burst activities can be carried out over one or more days if the timetable allows. If the timetable is more restrictive, the short burst activities could be taught intensely within a weekly slot by breaking the learning down into small, bite-sized chunks. The ten-minute activities can then be fitted in wherever the opportunity arises. By dividing up the curriculum in this way, the benefits of both approaches to science delivery can be capitalized upon. These considerations are in addition to the consideration of science being delivered within a cross-curricular topic or as a discrete science topic and to the extra time available for the consolidation of science through its use as a context within the literacy hour and/or numeracy lessons, as described in detail in Chapter 8.

Keeping a record of science

A focus throughout the book has been the need to ensure that scientific study builds on previous learning and that, for all pupils but especially the reluctant learners, teachers should be vigilant about not repeating activities, while nevertheless ensuring that there are opportunities for the consolidation of learning. It is therefore most important that the teacher keep records of both teaching and learning. Records of teaching show what the teacher has planned and delivered; records of learning record the learning that has taken place and, in turn, the achievements of his or her pupils.

Records of teaching

Records of teaching are not simply your planning records. Your planning will show what you intend to teach; records of teaching will show what you actually taught. The difference is important, as we often amend our teaching in response to assessments (see Chapter 10), in response to changes suggested by the pupils and in response to how we perceive a lesson to be heading. Records of teaching therefore ensure:

- that actual teaching is recorded, not the intended teaching;
- that pupils do not repeat the same scientific activities in subsequent classes;
- that pupils do not repeat the same scientific content at the same level in subsequent classes;
- a consideration of how pupils are grouped for science – particularly which groups work well together and are successful in their learning and which groups work less well together.

Records of teaching are most likely to take the form of original planning notes annotated with assessment notes and evaluations showing where the plans have been modified or adjusted. Records of teaching will also include records of the work carried out by the pupils, because not all pupils will carry out or complete all tasks, as they may be absent or the task may be differentiated and not consequently accessed by all pupils. These records will therefore demonstrate clearly the learning objectives that pupils have or have not experienced and/or completed in science. The records are only of use to subsequent teachers if they are passed on to the next teacher!

Records of learning

The recording of children's experiences in science and their resulting learning is an essential part of the assessment and evaluation process. Such records are used for a variety of purposes:

- to record actual learning that has taken place, rather than purely the intended learning;
- to record responses to tasks, in addition to outcomes of the task;

- to record performance in science, to be used as the starting point for future teaching and learning, through a record of session evaluations;
- to monitor pupil progress over time;
- to identify patterns and/or problems in learning;
- to provide an accurate and up-to-date profile of individual children's learning;
- to inform discussions with pupils about their learning, their progress, their future learning needs and their targets in science;
- to inform future teachers about a child's progress, needs, interests and capabilities;
- to facilitate effective transition within and between schools.

It can be appreciated that records of learning are dominated by assessment evidence and the interpretations of assessments made, as discussed in Chapter 10, including assessment data that are retained in the form of pieces of work, photographs of work and work in progress, and any comments made by adults on a pupil's learning. Additionally, the self-evaluations made by pupils form an important part of this record. This record then forms a record of both the pupils' learning in science *and* their attainment in science. It is important to put together this record and to maintain it for all the reasons listed above, but for reluctant learners it can also be used to motivate them in their future learning. Where the learner is reluctant as a result of low self-esteem, the sharing of this record of their progress over time may be the most motivating approach to re-engaging them in the curriculum that the teacher can take; indeed, the collating of a portfolio of work as part of the record of learning can be carried out with the learner, thus increasing his or her motivation to produce work to add to the collection.

This record of learning is most likely to consist of both formal and informal pieces of evidence. It is important that you adhere to the school's policy on records of learning (and teaching), but do accept that any form of evidence can be valid and add to the value of the record. On the other hand, remember that the record must be kept manageable and meaningful. It is therefore not just a case of photocopying and recording everything; you need to be discerning about what is being recorded and retained. The contents of the record are there to tell a story, the story of the pupil's developments in science over time.

Target setting in science

Target setting is a process that I have touched on throughout the book, and generates another type of record to be kept in science, although I believe it actually draws together many of the records you keep in science, including:

- records of assessment data;
- planning notes;
- references to the documentation for science;
- ideas for appropriate activities in science.

Target setting can be quite a simple process or quite a complicated one! At its simplest it is a record of intended learning for the pupil and his or her assessment results. At its most effective it uses attainment data and information about the known expectations of pupils of the same age to plan learning in science at an appropriate pace and an appropriate level for the pupil. Figure 17.1 is an important model for teachers to use to fully understand the target-setting cycle.

It is usual to set targets for a year, but the model may be used to set targets for longer or shorter intervals of time. The target-setting process generates another record that may aid reluctant learners to access the curriculum, by giving them an understanding of what learning is appropriate for their particular needs and ability. Indeed, the pupil may benefit, in terms of his or her self-esteem and engagement with the curriculum, from being involved in the target-setting process. For this to be a valid exercise, the pupil must:

- have an understanding of his or her own progress;
- have knowledge of his or her own record of learning;
- have knowledge of the expectations of his or her age group, through the sharing of learning outcomes or the level descriptions within the National Curriculum Order for Science;
- have an understanding of how he or she learns in science;
- have carried out self-evaluations of his or her own work.

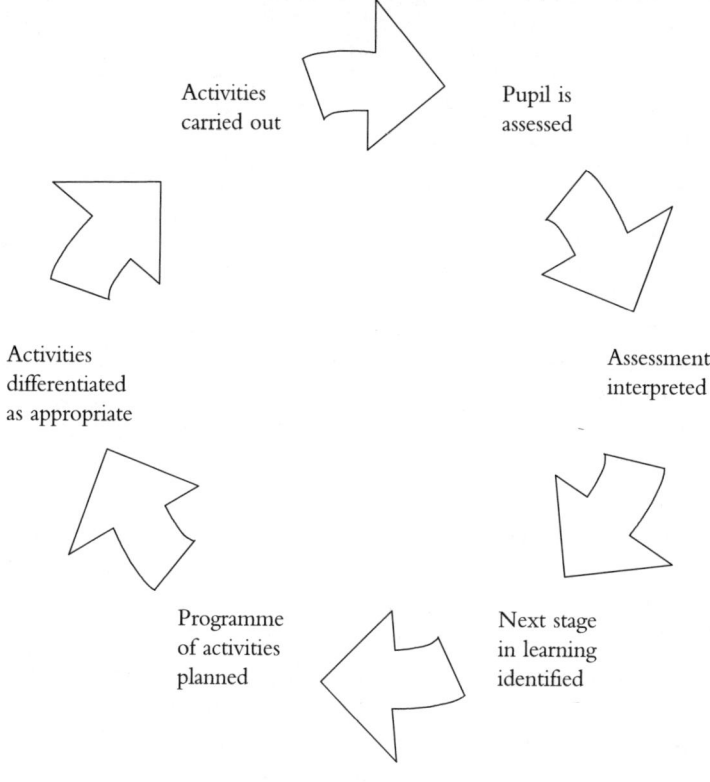

Figure 17.1 A model for target setting

18 Working with others

As has been noted throughout the book, science not only provides many opportunities for pupils to work with other pupils and with adults, but also is dependent on these opportunities for pupils to make sense of their learning. Science is therefore a social subject whose study is enhanced by discussion and sharing of ideas. It is this aspect that makes science an excellent vehicle for developing speaking and listening skills, together with the social skills of tolerance, empathy, cooperation and fairness, leading to an awareness and understanding of the needs of others. For reluctant learners it provides a context for their engagement with others and relevance for their study. Yet it must be remembered that working with others is a skill in itself. Pupils may not possess the skills needed, and these may then have to be taught. The skills needed may be broken down into the following:

- a willingness to work with others;
- an ability to present one's own ideas verbally;
- a willingness to listen to the contributions of others, without interruption, and to respond appropriately to the contributions of others;
- the ability to question critically the contributions of others;
- a willingness to verbally justify one's own ideas;
- preparedness to change or amend one's own views;
- preparedness to accept the views of others even if they differ from one's own views;
- an ability to compromise;
- openness to trying out others' suggestions.

Tasks and activities can be presented to develop and use these various skills.

It can be appreciated that, when approached appropriately, it enhances the science learning, whereas when not approached appropriately, it can result in diminished learning at best and disengagement at worst. It is therefore important that the teacher is aware of the skills needed and works towards ensuring that all pupils have these skills.

Working with peers

Working with peers has been touched on throughout the book, including a consideration within Chapter 13 of its benefits with respect to supporting the learning of others. As also noted throughout the book, I believe that working with peers is one of the most important strategies for studying science. When structured well, working with peers on scientific activities promotes:

- *teamwork* – the notion of working and learning together, benefiting from each other's ideas, explanations, suggestions and/or actions;
- *cooperation* – being able to agree courses of action;
- *efficiency of work* – sharing tasks fairly, agreeing the most effective way of working on an activity;
- *appreciation* – of the ideas of others, of the contributions of others;
- *open-mindedness* – the ability to consider other perspectives;
- *learning* – building on one's own ideas, taking on board the ideas of others and developing a wider understanding;
- *problem solving* – using discussions with others to consider various solutions to a problem.

The overriding benefit of working with peers is the opportunity to discuss ideas, to bounce ideas off each other, and to come to a shared understanding. It is these processes that truly help learners to make sense of their learning.

When you are planning for pupils to work with their peers, it is essential to consider the mix and size of the groups you will organize. For reluctant learners a large group may be intimidating or may provide an arena for them to disrupt the learning. A paired group may be more encouraging for a reluctant learner, although the teacher must be mindful of the reluctant learner's friends within the class, in order to avoid pairing the reluctant learner with a pupil he or she does not get on with! Groupings may be mixed ability or of similar ability, or they may be friendship groupings. Friendship groupings may work very well or the learning may be interrupted by conversations about areas other than the science task the group is involved in. Quite a dilemma for the teacher when arranging groupings! The key is to know your pupils well and know which groupings are profitable and which are not. This knowledge may have to be arrived at through trial and error, although discussions with previous teachers of the pupils will support your judgements.

It is often advised that groupings of three or four pupils are the optimum size. This group size allows for all ideas to be shared, whereas with larger groups it may take too much time for everyone to speak, and other members of the group may become restless. Moreover, within a paired group, if a disagreement arises, there are no other members to help resolve it. I use both paired groupings and larger groups, depending upon the task presented. I often use paired groups for discussions and research work, as I find the pupils who are willing to work in this way are eager to resolve their own differences and to benefit from each other's ideas. I use a group of three or four pupils for investigative work, where the sub-tasks can be *shared out*. I also form the groups in different ways:

- Allowing friendship groups or pairings – the pupils form their own groups (but are *warned* that if there are problems with the group I will not allow them to work together again!).
- Set groups – groups that I know work well together and are labelled with the name of a colour, for ease of organization.
- New groups – when I ask pupils to work with someone they've not worked with before. This is useful for trying out new combinations of pupils.
- Mixed-ability groups – when I want the more able pupils to support the learning of the less able.

I have heard of many other ways to form groups, from picking numbers out of a hat to grouping according to register number, but I prefer to group according to some criterion based on my knowledge of the pupils. Also, I do not make an issue of gender in the classroom, but if a group is three or four in number, I do expect a mixed-gender group to form. I am also mindful of the names that I give groups, as I do think that names have a psychological effect on the group (as studies have indeed shown). *The Great Green Group* and *the Intelligent Indigo Group* sound much more positive than Group A, Group B, etc.!

As with all teaching matters, it is important that the pupils know your intentions and expectations for the group task. If you are focusing on one of the skills for group work – for example, responses to the contributions of others – inform the group that this is what you will be looking for. It is also important to share the learning outcomes of the group work, so that the group are aware of why they are working together and the relevance of the task to their individual learning needs.

Do take time to establish an agreed code of conduct for working within a group. Indeed, it may be profitable to draw up this code with the pupils. The code will be based on the skills of group work: for example, not interrupting others and not making derogatory comments about the contributions of others. This is a valuable exercise for pupils who have the maturity to consider what is needed for effective group work and if group work is not proceeding as it should, the code can be consulted to identify where the problems arose.

Working with adults

I have considered the role of adults supporting learning in the classroom in Chapters 13 and 17, focusing on the attributes that the adult must have for the role and the skills the teacher needs for working with a range of adults in the classroom. It is important, when other adults are present in the classroom, that both the teacher in charge of the class and the pupils know how to respond to these adults who are involved in the learning process. Between the teacher and other adults, including teaching assistants, learning mentors, nursery nurses, adults providing specialist support, parents, volunteers and specialist teachers, there must be a professional relationship that is evident to the pupils. This establishes the status of the other adults in the classroom and implies validity in their role within learning. It is vital that all adults feel valued for their contributions and are fully aware of the expectations concerning their contributions. They must therefore be fully informed of the lesson, its contents and its intended outcome, and their own role within it. Almost all, if not all, schools have written policies or policy statements on adults in the classroom that cover issues such as the information they will require to be effective in the role, the code of conduct to be followed and the need to maintain confidentiality, all of which will aid teachers in working effectively with the range of adults now employed in schools. It is also essential to ensure that the boundaries of the role, and the responsibilities it carries, are clear to all – including the pupils.

The pupils' relationships with the adults other than the teacher in charge of the class need to be made explicit to the pupils. Adults must never be regarded as *helpers*; whether they are paid or unpaid, they are members of the teaching and learning team and are to be addressed as such. Pupils need to be aware that the adults are there to enhance the learning process through:

- supporting learning;
- facilitating group work;
- acting as experts;
- acting as interpreters of the curriculum.

I feel that the most important aspects of working with adults for the pupils is the development of social skills and the development of language, together with promoting learning and an enthusiasm for scientific study. Adults are in the unique position of being able to model the behaviours required and the *correct* language to use; they are able to use questioning and discussion well to scaffold pupils' learning and engender a true enthusiasm for the subject.

Part Eight

Resources for Science

Resources for science

There are so many resources for science that a consideration of resources is almost impossible to compile. What I am presenting are a set of appendices that set out my own favourite sources of support and resources in science.

Appendix 1 details the sources I have referred to within the body of the book, together with my top ten list of books for use in science lessons. In view of the vast number of science and science-related books that are on the market today, the restriction of a top ten lists ensures that I do not fill up the book with numerous titles of other books I have read or that have inspired me in science.

Within the book I have listed many website addresses, including a top ten for pupils. I use Appendix 2 to provide a top ten list of websites for teachers, although my personal top ten changes daily as I find even more interesting sites on offer.

I had intended to provide an appendix for scientific vocabulary, but this is too wide for an appendix even to be contemplated! I therefore use Appendix 3 to direct you towards dictionaries and glossaries you might find useful with your pupils.

Appendix 1: Reference list and other books

Reference list

Association for Science Education (2001) *Be Safe!*, 3rd edn. Hatfield: ASE.

The Concise Oxford Dictionary, 7th edn, ed. J. B. Sykes. Oxford: Oxford University Press.

Department for Education and Skills (2003) *Excellence and Enjoyment: A Strategy for Primary Schools*. London: DfES Publications.

Farmery, C. (2002) *Teaching Science 3–11: The Essential Guide*. London: Continuum.

Feasey, R. (1999) *Primary Science and Literacy*. Hatfield: Association for Science Education.

Harlen, W. (1992) *The Teaching of Science: Studies in Primary Education*. London: David Fulton.

Hodgson, B. and Scanlon, E. (1985) *Approaching Primary Science: A Reader*. London: Harper & Row.

Milne, A. A. and Shepherd, E. H. (1998) *A World of Winnie-the-Pooh*. London: Dean.

Qualifications and Curriculum Authority (1999a) *The National Curriculum: Handbook for Primary Teachers in England*. London: DfEE/QCA.

Qualifications and Curriculum Authority (1999b) *Early Learning Goals*. London: DfEE/QCA.

Qualifications and Curriculum Authority (2000) *Curriculum Guidance for the Foundation Stage*. London: DfEE/QCA.

Qualifications and Curriculum Authority (accessed August 2004) National Curriculum online. www.nc.uk.net/nc_resources/html/inclusion.

Rosen, M. (2000) *Centrally Heated Knickers*. London: Penguin.

Top ten list of useful books

The top ten is listed purely as a set of books I have used effectively, or intend to use, to support my teaching. The books are presented in no particular order.

1. Booth, G., McDuell, B. and Sears, J. (1999) *World of Science*. Oxford: Oxford University Press.
2. Hodgson, B. and Scanlon, E. (eds) (1985) *Approaching Primary Science: A Reader*. London: Harper & Row.
3. Wood, D. (1998) *How Children Think and Learn*, 2nd edn. Oxford: Blackwell.
4. Feasey, R. and Gallear B. (2000) *Primary Science and Numeracy*. Hatfield: Association for Science Education.
5. Goldsworthy, A. and Holmes, M. (1999) *Teach It! Do It! Let's Get to It!* Hatfield: Association for Science Education.
6. Naylor, S., Keogh, B. and Goldsworthy, A. (2004) *Active Assessment*. London: David Fulton in association with Millgate House Publishers.
7. Edwards, A. and Knight, P. (1994) *Effective Early Years Education: Teaching Young Children*. Buckingham: Open University Press.
8. Grey, D. (1999) *The Internet in School*. London: Cassell Education.
9. Dean, J. (1996) *Managing Special Needs in the Primary School*. London: Routledge.
10. Ward, A. (1989) *1000 Ideas for Primary Science*. London: Hodder & Stoughton.

Appendix 2: Useful websites for teachers

Top ten list of websites for teachers

1. www.qca.org.uk – the website of the Qualifications and Curriculum Authority. It provides a range of information about teaching and learning.
2. www.ncaction.org.uk – a website that provides samples of pupils' work levelled against the National Curriculum level descriptions. It provides commentaries about the work.
3. www.primaryresources.co.uk – a website that provides ideas for a range of activities, ideas for worksheets and ideas for assessments.
4. www.fearofphysics.com – a super website for explaining many of the concepts and theories in physics.
5. www.dfes.gov.uk – the website of the Department for Education and Skills. It provides information regarding the issues raised in this book and issues that may be raised in your classroom.
6. www.ase.org.uk – the website of the Association for Science Education. The ASE has provided the inspiration for my teaching in science over the years! The website provides a myriad of advice, advertises forthcoming events that teachers may be interested in, and has an excellent bookshop. If I could access only one website, this would be the one!
7. http://bubl.ac.uk/link/s/scientists.htm – a website providing the biographies of many scientists.
8. www.nakedscientist.com – an online radio show presented by the University of Cambridge. The website enables you to hear science, medicine and technology news, discoveries

and breakthroughs being discussed by scientists, together with various other information, ideas for science and interviews with modern-day scientists.

9. www.ask.co.uk – this is the address of the search engine Ask Jeeves. I use it regularly for finding information and for locating the answers to those tricky little questions we often have!

10. www.teachingideas.co.uk – a website similar to the primary resources website (number 3 above), as it presents ideas for activities, worksheets and assessments.

Appendix 3: Vocabulary, dictionaries and glossaries

Top ten list of books for science vocabulary, dictionaries and glossaries

1. Anderson, M. (2002) *A–Z of Key Concepts in Primary Science*. Exeter: Learning Matters.
2. Asimov, I. (ed.) (1974) *Words of Science and the History behind Them*. London: Harrap.
3. Burton, N. and Wright, L. (eds) (1998) *Signs and Symbols in Primary Science*. Hatfield: Association for Science Education.
4. *Concise Science Dictionary*, 2nd edition (1991). Oxford: Oxford University Press.
5. Craig, A. and Rosney, C. (1988) *The Usborne Science Encyclopedia*. London: Usborne.
6. *Encarta Essential Dictionary* (2002). London: Bloomsbury.
7. Feasey, R. (1998) *Primary Science Equipment*. Hatfield: Association for Science Education.
8. Mascull, B. (1997) *Key Words in Science and Technology*. London: HarperCollins.
9. Sutton, C. (1992) *Words, Science and Learning*. Milton Keynes: Open University Press.
10. Wellington, J. J. (1998) *Science Dictionary*. London: Questions Publishing Company.

Index